Praise for *Togetherness*

"*Our lives are defined by relationships—those that we have with ourselves, our bodies, and our past, as well as with our world and other people. In a responsible and practical manual that you'll want to keep at your fingertips, spiritual scholar Cyndi Dale and psychotherapist Andrew Wald draw upon their combined experience of over 30,000 client sessions and 50,000 therapy hours to give new meaning to this most fundamental experience of our lives. The Reflective Moments at the end of each chapter give us the powerful opportunity to experiment with our own relationships and discover how the principles identified in the book apply to our lives.*

If you've always known that there's more to your life experiences than you learned in 'Relationships 101,' this is the beautiful book you've been waiting for. For everyone from engineers to homemakers, from politicians to healers, this book opens the door to the source of your deepest beliefs and sheds new light on every choice you will ever make. I love this book!"

—**Gregg Braden**, New York Times best-selling author of *Deep Truth,*
  The Divine Matrix and Fractal Time

"*Togetherness goes directly to the heart of the matter, offering insights and practices that can be put to use immediately for deepening the intimacy and expanding the joy in every close relationship.*"

—**Peggy McColl**, New York Times best-selling author

"Togetherness *is not simply a relationship self-help book; it is a guide to living all our relationships as part of our journey toward personal and spiritual growth. Psychotherapist Andy Wald and Intuitive Consultant Cyndi Dale prove the perfect combination, illuminating their insights with real-life examples taken from their thousands of hours of client sessions, as well as their own lives. First they gently help us explore the personal misperceptions that can prevent us from believing in our own worthiness—a necessary preparation for 'togetherness with self.' Then they deftly help us explore the patterns and conditioning we bring into our relationships with others, and what it truly means to be 'together and yet alone' while in relationship. Finally, they guide us in an exploration of our relationship with the divine, and how our human relationships can come to be a reflection of our highest self. This is a beautiful yet practical book, exploring love and relationship with a depth few have managed."*

—Lisa Erickson, Buddhism editor for BellaOnline.com

"Togetherness *is a wonderful contribution on how to improve relationships, starting with ourselves, and moving on to our partner, and to the divine. We are given multiple examples of where people get stuck (on issues like money, sexuality, and infidelity) and are exposed to methods for looking within ourselves for answers, which include honoring ourselves and others, communicating consciously, and learning to dance through life with grace, depth, and appreciation for the gift of relationships!"*

—Brigitte Mars, author of *The Sexual Herbal*

"Togetherness *is a great and wonderful book on love and the possibility of love. Excellently written, it can be of use to those who wish to deepen and expand their knowledge of this eternal topic."*

—Rudolph Bauer, Ph.D., Diplomate in Clinical Psychology, A.B.P.P. Co-Director, The Washington Center for Consciousness Studies. Editor, *Transmission: The Journal of the Awareness Field*

"The most important relationship is the one with Self. Cyndi Dale and Andrew Wald take that core truth and weave a deep yet clear understanding of how that expands and interacts with all other relationships into the beauty of our self-creation. Finally, a book that expands the consciousness of who we are!"

—**Dee Wallace**, actress, healer, and author of *Bright Light: Spiritual Lessons from a Life in Acting*

"*Togetherness is a beautiful roadmap for opening one's eyes and heart to the essential love that is all around us. While Dale and Wald approach their subject from differing professional backgrounds, they share a deep reverence for one of life's most soul-stirring experiences: the expression of personal love. In addition to meaningful meditations at the end of each chapter, the authors use examples from their respective practices, literature, and, most generously, their own lives, to illustrate the power of love to both transform and heal. This is a wonderful book.*"

—**Suzanne Guillette**, author of *Much To Your Chagrin*

"*Thank you Cyndi Dale and Andrew Wald for writing* Togetherness—*it is a powerful and precious book that explores intimate love with the self, with another, with community and with the Divine. Examining our insecurities and our humanness,* Togetherness *explores the quality of intimacy that brings the deep connection we all yearn for. This book tells stories about how everyday people find the love that is a catalyst for their growth and transformation. And it will help you manifest and attract your heart's deepest desire by weaving together practical action steps and spiritual perspectives.*"

—**Nancy Lindgren**, interfaith minister and energy healer

"Being together is the heart of our journey here as human beings. Togetherness—to be in relationship, whether with oneself, with others, or with the Divine energies, is what writes your spirit upon the world, and what builds your soul through time. With their deep insights and accessible writing, Cyndi Dale and Andrew Wald have provided almost a step-by-step guide into working this profound and at times cryptic magic of healthy joyful relationship into your present-day real life. Togetherness is an essential book for anyone who calls themselves a human being."

—**Holly Long,** songwriter, recording artist

"With great compassion and sensitivity, Cyndi Dale and Andrew Wald guide us through the emotional minefields and contradictions of the human psyche that sabotage relationships. Togetherness shows how to defuse our deepest fears that we are not worthy of love and illuminates the way to connection with ourselves, others, and the divine."

—**Miriam Knight**, publisher of New Consciousness Review

"Togetherness helps teach us to love others where they stand, but more importantly that love needs to begin with the self… for there is no separation. Difficult to understand and put in practice, especially in stressful times, but Cyndi Dale and Andrew Wald provide a clear path to follow."

—**K. Paul Stoller, M.D.**, FACHM, author of Oxytocin: The Hormone of Healing and Hope

"Relationships are complex and challenging at the best of times, but when they work and flow we receive their infinite gifts. Togetherness does not promise a cure-all but it does provide a grounded, well-laid-out guide to creating and maintaining solid connections with self and others and celebrating the most precious of all gifts...that of love."

—**Lucinda Drayton**, composer and singer of the spiritual classic
  A Hundred Thousand Angels

"Togetherness is the culmination of the shared desire of Andy Wald and Cyndi Dale to co-create a book that could blend the very best of their respective beliefs and practices in their work with couples. The common ground they have found in their book is the transformation of the frustration and pain that often erodes intimate relationships after the initial infatuation, after we touch a deeper happiness that is our whole reason for seeking love in the first place. The result is a fine book that reflects their enthusiastic and pragmatic conviction that couples can 'get it right.' Making relationships work requires a dedication and determination to change the way we think about and behave in relationships. Togetherness is just such a theory and practice manual, but it is also infused with the love that one feels in the presence of the authors.

Although Andy and Cyndi work and live in uniquely different ways, they have felt a tremendous simpatico since their professional paths crossed ten years ago. I remember Andy's enthusiasm in telling me he had met this wonderful intuitive counselor while visiting with his wife's family in Minneapolis. When I asked him how he would describe the essence of Cyndi, he said, 'She's one in a million.' I feel the same way about this book, and I'm glad the stars aligned so they could meet and write this wonderful guide to staying in love."

—**Harry Rieckelman**, LCSW-C, Certified Imago Couples Therapist

"Cyndi Dale and Andrew Wald have written an exceptionally moving and inspiring book—one that will show you how to care for the soul of each of your most important relationships, starting with the one you have with yourself."

—**Cathy Ladman**, comedian, actor, writer

"With their new book, Togetherness, Cyndi Dale and Andrew Wald have created a jewel: In lyrical language they explore the human journey deepening our compassion for the self, our capacity to be separate from and connected to others, and our capacity to feel connected to the Divine. Through clear discussion, stories about their clients' lives, and exercises in self-reflection, they draw us into the most essential of all human quests—the longing to feel worthy of love and to give love."

—**Anne C. Mazonson**, M.D.

TOGETHERNESS

TOGETHERNESS
Creating and Deepening Sustainable Love

CYNDI DALE
ANDREW WALD
with Debra Evans

Designed by Anthony J.W. Benson and Anthony Sclavi
Cover photo: *The Dance* by Jerry Downs — jerrydownsphoto.com
Cyndi Dale photo by Sasha M Zukanoff
Andrew Wald photo by Bryan Blanken at Freed Photography
Edited by Debra Evans

Printed in the UNITED STATES OF AMERICA
    ISBN: 978-1-937061-85-2
    Library of Congress Control Number: 2011930662

Published jointly by:
        Deeper Well Publishing
        and
        BRIO
        12 South 6th Street, Suite 1250
        Minneapolis, MN 55402

        For press inquiries, email: publicity@deeperwellpub.com

The minute I heard my first love story,
I started looking for you, not knowing
how blind that was.

Lovers don't finally meet somewhere,
they're in each other all along.

-Jalal ad-Din Rumi
(translated by Coleman Barks)

CONTENTS

NOTE TO THE READER

This book was born out of the professional respect and personal admiration and gratitude that we—your authors, Cyndi Dale and Andrew Wald—have for one another. For several years, we have enjoyed a depth of conversation with each other where we have "compared notes" on life, love, parenting, spiritual growth, and the joys of working with people through our respective modalities (between the two of us, an amalgamation of psychotherapeutic, intuitive, energetic, and spiritual approaches).

When it came time to turn our vision for this book into a reality, we found that the most natural way to cull from our own experiences and meld our ideas and stories was to be interviewed by our writing partner, Debra Evans. As Debra laid out maps for our many discussions and asked the questions that got us rolling each time we gathered, we were free to let the ideas flow. It was an experience of creative togetherness where the hours always flew by like minutes.

In determining the tone and feel we wanted this book to have, all three of us were clear that we wanted to extend the experience and spirit of being in conversation to you as well—to basically *continue* the conversation with our readers. As the topic of togetherness is about a depth of connection and closeness that transforms, we felt that communicating with soulfulness, authenticity, and vulnerability would have to take precedence over professional decorum or distance.

The overall narrative voice of the book is a reflection of this informal interview style. In the weaving of ideas, practices, and stories, we have chosen to alternate between speaking in *one voice*, as a "we" (when discussing topics that are relevant to all of us as women and men or to the two of us as the primary authors) to speaking in *two voices* (what Andy has to say versus Cyndi, or what "he" says and what "she" says).

To avoid confusion when writing about our clients or sharing experiences from our own lives, we have opted to identify ourselves as "Andy" or "Cyndi" respectively. When you arrive at passages where you read things like "Andy's client…" or "Cyndi's partner…," please know that neither of us has temporarily stepped out of the book. Given the nature of co-authoring, this is our way of clarifying exactly whose experience or perspective is being described, when making that distinction is important to the ideas being presented.

Stories from our clients' lives and loves are shared throughout to illuminate the topics at hand, and in each case we have either left their names out of the story or changed their names to protect their anonymity.

We hope you will enjoy reading this book as much as we enjoyed writing it.

PROLOGUE
LOVE IS ACHIEVABLE

How many times have you wished that you had a manual that would show you exactly how to build a relationship that works? Or a map that would help you to find your way through the twists and turns of intimate relationships? Perhaps you've read other books about relationships but still find yourself searching for something more—information, skills, or understanding that will help you to either find or sustain a happy and strong relationship.

Or maybe you would simply like to read a book that will leave you feeling optimistic and excited about relationships; that will remind you of the thing that often gets obscured in the midst of our busy lives...

Loving relationships are *a wonderment*. Loving each other, sharing life together, growing and evolving together—it is all so incredible!

We do tend to forget this, don't we? The enchantment gets rather lost and complications set in. That is why we, your authors, have written this book. Combining our many years of professional experience, we're eager to offer a guidebook that demystifies relationships without taking the soul out of them. Merging psychological and spiritual perspectives, our intention is to provide readers with time-tested antidotes to some of the most persistent and painful challenges we face in sharing our lives with others.

The decision to write this book came after a series of conversations between us where we kept returning to the same two baseline issues in relationships. Although we in no way wish to oversimplify the complexity of intimate relationships, there are two beliefs that are particularly problematic and that seem to underlie many of the troubles that people experience in matters of love. These are commonly shared beliefs that impact people from every walk of life, no matter how caring, intelligent, well-educated, psychologically astute, or spiritually aware a person is. Somewhere along the way, many of us made the determination that we're not worthy of being loved. We may not be able to explain *why* we're not worthy; we simply believe that we are not.

That is misguided belief #1.

Then comes misguided belief #2.

Each of us goes through our own set of challenges and heartbreaks, and we watch some of the people around us wrestle with their personal and relational issues. Little by little, we may come to the conclusion that fulfilling love really isn't achievable—so why try? Whether single or in a partnership, a decision is made: Give up the quest and settle for the way things are. Some of us might recall making the decision consciously (stating something along the lines of "That's *it*! I'm done!"). But for the majority of us, this sad conclusion is arrived at gradually, almost imperceptibly.

Over time, doubt, disappointment, and resignation can take a great toll, and too many relationship dreams get pushed to the side; often replaced by work, money concerns, parenting, and other day-to-day responsibilities. "The dream" gets eclipsed by "the grind."

And all because of misguided beliefs and misperceptions!

But we want you to take heart, because beliefs and perceptions can be changed, and that is what we will address in the pages of this book. Through the weaving of stories (both from our clients' lives and our own), practices, inner reflections, and action steps, we will invite you to consider new possibilities for yourself, all the while reminding you of a truth that reaches deeper than any belief can ever go:

You were *born* worthy.

You are worthy of closeness; worthy of tenderness; worthy of extraordinary love.

Not only were you born worthy, there is nothing you need to do (or can do) to maintain your worthiness or earn more of it. Your worthiness is total and complete.

And it gets even better. You also don't have to wait to fully understand and accept that you are worthy before you can have the relationship you want. Page by page, chapter by chapter, you can instead let a gentle transformation occur—whatever kind of transformation you're looking for. If a lack of self-love or a distrust of intimate relationships has limited you, we're passionate about helping you to break free of those limitations. If you're already in a strong relationship, we're excited to show you how to make it even better.

Why Togetherness?

No matter what phase of life or relational circumstances any of us find ourselves in right now, love matters. Whether young, middle-aged, or old; whether single, married, or on the fence about a relationship, love matters. Even if we're hard pressed to define or describe what love is, we know that it is our fuel. When allowed to flow, love delights the body. It nourishes the heart. It nurtures the soul.

As far as we can tell, loving is more an art than a science. Although we could ponder the universal and phenomenological nature of love, what we have found is that what really touches and moves people is the *personal* expression of love.

When it comes to love, most of us want closeness, tenderness, affection, and intimacy. What most of us desire is to be accepted, appreciated, wanted, and cherished. In addition to our needs for water, oxygen, and food, what we most seem to hunger for is the emotional depth and heart-to-heart connection that we have made the focal point of this book—and that connection is *Togetherness*.

Togetherness, which we explore in detail throughout the book, is the love that truly nourishes and sustains us. Individually and collectively, and through all stages and circumstances, togetherness is the bond we share with life, love, and one another.

As we contemplated its impact and significance, we determined that there are **Four Cornerstones** of togetherness that you may find important and useful at different junctures in your life. As the following outline describes, when your relationship needs and priorities change, togetherness is right there with you.

The Four Cornerstones of Togetherness

- **Togetherness within the Self** – when you want to claim your inherent worthiness

- **Togetherness with a Future Partner** – when you want to open your heart to transformative intimacy

- **Togetherness with a Current Partner** – when you want to nourish and sustain the love you already have

- **Togetherness with the Divine** – when you long to deepen the bonds of faith, love, and spirit

We have divided the book into four sections that illuminate the *Four Cornerstones* and how they can support you in your unique journey of love and awakening. In this way, *Togetherness* is a relationship book for literally everyone. Although there is a distinct focus here on attracting and joyfully maintaining intimate relationships between couples, there is nearly equal weight given to the love of oneself, the love of "soul mates" that appear as friends, family members, or other close companions, and the relationship between you and the Divine.

A Matter of Perception
In the book *A Course in Miracles*, it's stated that transformation is a shift in perception. In other words, profound and lasting change is possible in an instant, arriving as an awareness or recognition from within the self. With that possibility in mind, each chapter is intentionally written to spark your own shifts in perception—shifts that can serve to transform all of your relationships, romantic and otherwise.

In our professional practices (Andy's psychotherapy and Cyndi's intuitive counseling), an essential aspect of what we provide for our clients is the chance to slow down and make the shift from being reactionary to being reflective. Aiming to bring a similar quality of spaciousness to the experience of reading this book, at the conclusion of each chapter, you'll come to a *Reflective Moment*—a meditative pause to reflect on the conversation at hand and to tune into your inner wisdom.

The Reflective Moment is an awareness practice that was also inspired by a powerful dream that Cyndi had two nights in a row. In the dream, Cyndi was walking along a sandy beach and deep in thought. "What's my purpose?" she asked herself over and over again.

"What is my purpose?"

Lining the beach was a long string of one-story office and retail buildings. A man, one of the shopkeepers, thanked Cyndi for the help and healing she provided to people through her work. Touched by his appreciation, she thanked him and continued on her walk.

Eventually, and much to her surprise, she found her own store amidst all the other stores! She quickly noticed that hers was the smallest of them all. It was a tiny little diner with just a few booths and counter stools. And its size wasn't the only oddity about it; laying on the small countertop was a pair of pink glasses.

Intuitively, Cyndi understood that these were God's glasses. The pink color was a merging of red (representing our real needs as human beings) and white (representing our spiritual values). These pink-rimmed spectacles provided an objective yet heart-filled view of any person or situation. When she put them on for the first time, Cyndi understood that whenever she or her customers at the diner would wear the glasses, they would have the ability to ask the question, "How does God see me right now?" and to receive the life-altering answer to that question. Viewing themselves through the eyes of divine love, shame and self-judgment would be seen for what they are. Unhealthy misperceptions. Observing themselves with true compassion, past mistakes, failures, and losses would be understood and accepted. In the healing light of awareness, fear would lose its power, defensive walls would come down, and love would have the opportunity to flourish.

People would come to the diner for a meal, but they would leave with a new lease on life. They might start off chomping on a cheese-burger and fries, and then God's glasses would get passed around the diner—and suddenly everything would be different. Instantly, they would have a shift in perception related to something that had been confounding them just moments before.

This dream points to something that we, your authors, believe is possible for you in any given moment—a clearer view of yourself, your life, and your relationships that is thoroughly uplifting and surprisingly beautiful.

And finally, a special message to those of you who specifically want to find love or want to heal a relationship that is currently in a state of turmoil: Our hope is that you know and trust that love is achievable for you—and if you don't know it yet, that you come to know it very soon. No matter how much frustration, pain, or loss you may have experienced in your relationships, we know with certainty that togetherness can *fully* restore hope, optimism, and joy in your life. We have seen the ideas contained in this book work wonders for thousands of clients, and we have faith that they will do the same for you.

Andrew Wald and Cyndi Dale
Spring 2012

CORNERSTONE I
Togetherness within the Self

THE FIRST CORNERSTONE of togetherness is the
relationship with oneself. The bedrock of all relationships
is the one we cultivate and tend to internally, reflected
in how we perceive ourselves, how we talk to ourselves
in the privacy of our interior world, and the choices we
make regarding the way we live our lives. Within the
first four chapters that comprise Part I, you will have an
opportunity to get emotionally current with yourself by
exploring where you've been, where you are now, and
where you want to go. Along the way, you can uncover
beliefs and perceptions that may be impinging on your
deepest satisfaction; reclaim forgotten aspects of yourself;
melt away old remnants of fear and shame; clarify your
personal boundaries; and discover how claiming your
inherent worthiness is the entry point to happy and
fulfilling relationships.

CHAPTER 1
THE SEARCH FOR A SOUL MATE

Life has taught us that love does not consist in gazing
at each other, but in looking outward together.
–ANTOINE DE SAINT-EXUPERY

You are the star of a great love story. And whether or not you realize it, you have already become someone great through your quest for love. Think of the courage, strength, vulnerability, willingness, and faith love has required of you. Think of the times that love has asked you to step into the unknown with no guarantee of what the outcome would be. Your journey of the heart has shaped you in countless ways, giving way to the person you now know yourself to be.

Because the ups and downs of relationships are experienced and felt in such a personal way, we believe it's worthwhile to remind you that you are not alone. As an intuitive counselor (Cyndi) and a psychotherapist (Andy), we have tallied the numbers and compared notes. Between the two of us, we have engaged in more than 80,000 client sessions over the past 35 years, many of which have centered on the pain, confusion, longing, and hopes for a relationship. We have plumbed the depths with thousands of people who were either looking to attract their dream relationship, fix one that is broken, nourish

28

the one they love, or figure out how to navigate the turbulent waters of ending one.

On a personal level, we too have lived the quest—the search for that special someone. As far as we can tell, it appears to be one of the greatest quests of a lifetime.

Along the path of love, where would you locate yourself right now? Perhaps you're single and would describe yourself as an optimist who is determined to get it right next time, or maybe you're already in love, seeking to keep the love you have now burning long and bright. Or, single or partnered, perhaps you have quietly given up on love and are drawn to this book by a desire to believe in love again.

In any case, you are in the right place. Love has beckoned you forward all the days of your life, even in moments of weariness and doubt…and it will not let you down now.

Each one of us has stories to tell. We are the curators of the loves and losses that have led us inexorably to the place we find ourselves in right now. Cyndi is a single mother enjoying the dating scene, allowing time to disentangle herself from a former relationship so that the bow is clean and neat. Her needs are gratefully met with friendships brimming with love. Andy has been happily married since 1973, and he believes in living what he espouses in his office. They are both devoted to the idea and ideal of this book: togetherness, whether it is found in singlehood, dating, or marriage, is worth the quest.

Whether you are with your life mate, still seeking a partner, or feeling stuck in a downward spiral with a current other, what we most want you to know is this:

You are worthy of a soul mate or true love—a relationship that embraces the full definition of love.

By any name or designation, soul mates are the people who validate our existence and elevate who we are. Through them, we are given the gift of coming to know ourselves. Think of the people you are closest to and you can see that they are the historians of your life, the keepers of your stories. And you are this for them as well. In each other's reflections, you see that your lives have importance, that they matter.

This depth of connection and bonding includes relationships labeled as husband, wife, spouse, companion, partner, significant other, and also those with people we call friend, acquaintance, mentor, parent, sibling, guide, daughter, son, and more. It encompasses the individuals we have known and those we've yet to meet.

Sometimes it's a matter of timing and choice that renders a soul mate more like a brother or sister than a lover. Cyndi's needs are met through her dear friends, men and women, who she knows to be her soul mates, or as she calls them, spirit mates. There is a particularly tight-knit group of women friends she playfully refers to as her "sister-friends." Their bond of intimacy is for the rest of their lives—one that strengthens, nourishes, and delights them. Similarly, Andy has treasured friends whom he has known even longer than his wife Tess, people who have been witness to the unfolding of his life over time.

Soul mates. The term has a resonance that extends even further, reaching beyond the everyday into the celestial, to incorporate our relationship with God, whoever you name that Higher Power who so believes in you and your deservedness of love.

The truth is that the strength, existence, or viability of a one-on-one relationship is actually dependent on the quality of all our relationships, including the ones we have with ourselves, others, and God.

Perhaps this inclusive view of relationships can serve to take some of the pressure off of romantic love. So even if you don't currently have a life partner, by creating love in the other areas of your life, you improve your chances of attracting and sustaining a relationship with a true life mate. It also offers a ray of hope, assuring that if you're in a relationship that has become dim or dreary, it can transform. It will start to sparkle and shine or it will end, allowing you to find an enduring and endearing love elsewhere. And if you're in a solid partnership already, you will be thrilled when you begin to see possibilities for even greater passion and deeper love than you've ever imagined.

Very often, people who are either nearing the end of life or have had a near-death experience report that they have seen the light. They know without a shadow of a doubt that what matters most is the love they have given and the love they have allowed themselves to receive. They decide, whether given one more hour or another forty years, they will no longer settle for anything less than love that heals, uplifts, and transforms. With the meaning of their life in focus, they become devoted to the kind of love that opens its arms and greets life with a full and grateful embrace.

The love within togetherness.

This is the type of love that we as your authors, your guides, and your fellow learners, are here to help you discover. This is the love that will help you love your life even while you are manifesting the love of your life. This is the love within togetherness, for at its root, togetherness is the central core and the eventual outcome of love. Love is a concept that is so big it becomes hard to grasp. Togetherness is love *in action*—it's the demonstration of love that helps us to see it, touch it, and feel its presence.

Feeling Lost About Love

Love is not easy to define—or obtain—even though nearly every book, song, movie, and even Internet site, at some level, is about the search for love. It can also be hard to recognize the love that comes knocking at your door when you don't know what it looks like. As young people, we're essentially told to go out there and love—just have a relationship, make it so. It's not surprising that we would end up making at least a few colossal messes by walking blindly into relationships with little understanding of the power we wield with our bodies, hearts, and minds. We don't learn how to have successful relationships in school, nor by looking to popular culture or the media for inspiring examples. In addition, many of us don't learn how to know love and trust in love at home when we're growing up.

When it comes to knowing and understanding love, we can get a bit lost. There are so many ways to define love, and so many things called love that are not—it's little wonder we flounder when it comes to understanding, finding, or creating love, especially that all-desirable "Relationship."

Ah, that "Relationship" with a capital "R." To find one or keep one, we've all done at least a few of the following: dated, married, stayed married unhappily, divorced, married again, had an affair, lived through someone else's affair, attended therapy, made our partner go to therapy, tried living together, done serial monogamy, or given up and bought a dog or hamster. We've all been there. The trouble is that love is so MUCH. It's so big, it's so huge, it has so many dimensions that it's hard to figure love out, much less create the ideal love relationship.

The Oak and the Acorn: Bonds of Connection
Rather than approaching love like a Rubik's Cube to be figured out, manipulated, and locked into place, we can look to the great oak tree to *unlock* love's mystery.

Love has much in common with the mighty oak of the forest. It is as hard to hold love in your hands, as it is to clasp your arms around a tree. How can you wrap your mind around something with so many components and corresponding effects? With the oak, there are the branches with fluttering leaves, which shelter life and provide shade; the graceful trunk, through which life-giving sap flows; the bark, which protects and shields. Love is like this too, providing shelter, protection, and nourishment for the soul, but still it seems unfathomable.

Like the oak, love's ability to endure the ravages of war, weather, and time itself is an indicator that something extraordinary is afoot. Attempting to discover the mystery of its origins—the truth of its source—has captivated lovers, poets, parents, and philosophers through the ages.

However, it turns out that there IS a way to really understand love, a wonderfully simple way.

At the core of the oak tree is the acorn, a clever little nut carrying a very big life force. The perfect symbol for togetherness, an acorn *can* be held in your hand, yet it holds the seed that contains all the information it needs to become a fully formed tree. Forever unified in their cycles and patterns of life, the microcosm of the acorn reflects the macrocosm of the oak.

The acorn is the intimate expression of the grandeur of the great tree. The same is true of togetherness. Togetherness is the intimate expression of love's immensity. Togetherness enables us to access the universal force of love so that we can share it in ways that are particularly meaningful and beautiful to those we are loving. In fact, the path between the beginning and the final resolution of a relationship—the naming of it as acquaintanceship, friendship, ally, lover, co-parent, or soul mate—is a walk of togetherness, a walk that is unique to those on its path.

Togetherness invites us into an intimacy that is close and tender by its very nature. While love can cruise at 35,000 feet, togetherness is right here, holding your hand. It is the magic that enables life-long companions to perceive the other's wrinkles as poems. When a relationship is based on togetherness, whether it's a marriage, parent-child relationship, or a friendship, tears are as precious as pearls. In fact, a full range of emotions is welcome. Our joys are as important to the other as their joys are to us. We see the other as having faults, but not constantly being at fault; having defects, but not being defective. When we feel together with and connected to another, it's easier to reveal all that we are—the good, the bad, and the unbelievable.

Togetherness is what was experienced between Winnie the Pooh and Piglet, the tiniest of them all, when Piglet sidled up to Pooh and took his hand.

"Pooh!" he whispered.

"Yes, Piglet."

"Nothing," said Piglet, taking Pooh's paw.

"I just wanted to be sure of you."

As Piglet understood, love isn't about appearance, form, shape, virtue, background, education, or intellect. Within love lays togetherness, a knowing and attentive connection that feels just right to the soul.

Together with Another

While a "couple" of any sort will spend most of their time walking side by side, autonomous but connected, each must be able to occasionally *hold* the other. At times, we will alternately find ourselves carrying the other or being carried; sometimes leading, sometimes following. The sign of real love, however, is that we carry each other within our hearts no matter which way the pendulum is swinging.

Some people believe that friendships, dating relationships, even family relations are "training wheels" for the final, big achievement: a true love. A reverse statement might be just as true, however. Learning how to be with a mate also teaches us how to relate to everyone else. The eventual conclusion is the same: We come to know ourselves *as* love, capable of loving one and all from the depth of our being.

Together within Oneself

Have you ever come to the end of a relationship and wondered, "What was that all about?" The relationship turns out to be less like a romance and more like a wake up call, a cup of coffee in the morning meant to entice us out of a cozy complacency. One of Cyndi's relationships wasn't even about an "us." It was a call for both partners to look in the mirror, understand themselves better, and evolve. Cyndi played her familial role of caretaker, or "taking on" all the care of a relationship to the point that she was right back in her childhood days of being one of the most flaming codependents one could ever meet. Codependency involves forgetting ourselves in the pursuit of pleasing another. That stage of the relationship came to an inevitable wall, with more than a few feathers flying, and she has since only spent time with men who are friends first—and friend second, as well.

Paradoxically, togetherness starts within oneself. The one who seeks to merge with another must be willing, at times, to be alone, although not to be confused with lonely. Sometimes when we're alone we're better able to face issues head-on and prepare ourselves internally for companion love. Although not in a romantic relationship, Cyndi derives an amazing sense of self and strength from raising her children with her ex-husband and being bonded with men and women friends alike. We learn a little more every time we surrender to the lessons of love, whether those lessons come to us while single or partnered. Everyone benefits when we *learn* from our lessons, becoming more empowered and emotionally available to love.

Sometimes we strive too hard to maintain the form of a relationship and miss the lessons altogether. Maybe we're dead-set on remaining single. Or, maybe we're steadfastly determined to keep a marriage together. For instance, Andy once worked with a woman who would do anything she could to hang on to her marriage. Her togetherness was all about being with this particular man, even though he cheated on her repeatedly.

One part of her, her heart, knew the truth, but she refused to listen to it.

"Janie!" her heart shouted, "He's not in love with you!"

Her mind, though, wanted this person to be her mate and clung desperately to the relationship.

This inner disharmony between her mind and her heart created dis-equilibrium; she was angry and heartsick. With Andy's help, she finally created a meeting ground for her mind and heart to come together after decades of estrangement. Once this long-awaited reunion took place, she was able to release her husband with love and find peace within herself. She figured out that her marriage helped her in that it showed her that she had abandoned herself. Once she achieved a state of internal harmony, she didn't need to cling to an unhealthy relationship. This is an example of the truth setting someone free.

Somewhere inside, we all know the truth. We may not want to admit it (for months, years, or even decades), but we do know when the circumstances of our relationship are right and when they're not. We just need to have the skills to understand ourselves better and a little more courage to face what we know to be true.

Janie's story vividly illustrates one of the primary forms of togetherness, the marriage between our head and our heart. Sometimes combining the two may feel like trying to combine oil and water; neither wants to mix with the other. However, if you're open and patient to hear what both parts have to say, a basic truth will emerge. Although you may not like or feel comfortable with the truth that emerges, if you accept it, you will find your clarity, integrity, and inner strength growing by leaps and bounds.

Some people are so afraid of relationships that they place the majority of their attention on themselves alone. They feel safe inside an emotionally protective cocoon, where life seems more predictable, simpler, or at least quieter. For them, the key is connecting more externally. By joining groups, making friends, and being out in the world, they may become open to a variety of relationships, even that special relationship with another.

There are other points in our lives when trying to find or enjoy a special someone is anything but enjoyable, such as when we're recovering from an illness or an addiction. At those times, we are so focused inward that we don't have the energy to put into an external relationship. Or if we're in a relationship, it can be rather one-sided. That's okay because there may be times when the situation is reversed and it will be lopsided the other way. People are able to give at different times depending on the situation. That is why it's best not to measure. It's rarely 50-50.

In addition, there are other times when it may be best to hold off on looking for a relationship if not currently in one, such as when we are so pre-occupied with meeting a goal or managing a challenging transition that we don't have extra energy to spare (i.e., we're in school, going through a divorce, or learning how to single parent). And even then, we need to be responsible and mindful of the relationships we do have, with friends and loved ones, by touching bases when we can. A brief phone call, a short email, half an hour together at a café—any of these can be a way to ensure that the garden of our relationships doesn't get overgrown with weeds while we're busy achieving our goals.

When we find ourselves working too hard to come to a decision about a relationship, sometimes the best thing to do is wait.

"Is he my soul mate? Is she the woman of my dreams?"

"Are we really meant to be good friends instead of lovers?"

"If I end the relationship, will it be the greatest regret of my life?"

Important questions like these can occupy a very large part of our mental activity, and ironically, can even get in the way of hearing the answer. The bigger the question, the greater the opportunity to slow down, wait, and listen for a prompting from our soul.

Many people mistakenly believe that relationships need to last forever in order to be considered successful. The truth is, not all relationships are intended to last forever. Even brief relationships can be considered valuable and successful if both people learn and grow from their time together. As current divorce statistics reflect, many relationships do grow apart. We would like to think that we always grow together, at the same time, pace, and in the same direction. But, there are times when that doesn't happen and it's no one's fault. For instance, some "best friends forever" that start in grade school find that in high school or college their interests differ and their friendship loses steam. In nature, you will often see a tree that starts out as one trunk then diverges into two trunks that grow in different directions, each searching for the light in its own way.

Togetherness with the Source

The Divine can move at any time and in any way. Although holding a vision for the relationship we want is important, how and when it comes to pass may take us by surprise. We might be in one of those transitional stages mentioned above or somehow preoccupied when we meet that "right" someone. Real love has its own mysterious timeline. That is why it's helpful to understand that togetherness is credited to something bigger than our individual ideas and plans.

In moments of unexpected grace, many of us have experienced what is referred to as a state of oneness, where our very consciousness seems to merge with everything and everyone else. Religions and spiritual traditions have taken many roads to describe and validate this sacred integration—where there is no separation between ourselves, others, and the Source of all that is.

As love is our very nature, we feel more like ourselves—we feel more *real*—when we give it. We are on this planet to create more love. We are designed to take that which is unformed and grow it into love. Likewise, we know innately how to take that which is malformed, untwist it, and grow it into love too. Our challenging feelings, including fear, anger, sadness, rage, loneliness, shame, jealousy, and other so-called negatives, are only underdeveloped states of love and joy. Our negative beliefs about ourselves, such as being unworthy, unlovable, undeserving, powerless, bad, or lacking in value, can be stepping-stones on the path to self-love.

As we surrender the various beliefs that have weighed us down, we can transform, just like a butterfly that has been released from its cocoon. It doesn't drag its cocoon around with it forevermore, no matter how essential it had been to the process of change. The butterfly's transformation includes the ability to freely use its wings, to freely move on—grateful for the gifts of the past but entirely unencumbered by them.

However, releasing the cocoon of old beliefs and limiting stories about relationships takes time, usually more than we'd like to think. The idea of "Mr. or Mrs. Right" can be tenacious. If we're willing to be radically honest, we will admit that many of us harbor the secret belief that there is only one person in the world for us and we just have to find them. Once we find them (or free ourselves from our current partner so they can find us!), we will be loved just the way we desire—and a relationship will finally become easy.

This matrix of beliefs is often an indicator that we're stuck in the habit of longing; a habit that takes us out of what we *do* have. No matter how much money or material success we may enjoy, this pattern of thinking keeps us living in a state of deprivation. It keeps us on a continual search for the love that we feel has abandoned us, but is actually all around us.

In the pages to follow, one of the opportunities set before you is freedom from this habit of longing. Not the sacred longing that fuels us in the search for meaning, but the forlorn kind of longing that turns toxic; the unquenchable thirst that keeps us locked into the lie that we don't *have* enough and we will never *be* enough.

There's no getting around it: Our past is part of us, always affecting our relationships. But that doesn't need to be a problem. Our burdens can be our blessings. Settling and suffering can be over. Through awareness, we can choose whether the impact of our past is detrimental or uplifting. We can choose to deepen the internal and external bonds that honor, nurture, and sustain love. We can be free to love and be loved—and the search for our soul mates can become one of our greatest and most delightful adventures.

A Reflective Moment

Think of the term "soul mate," allowing yourself to see, feel, and sense what these words bring forth in you.

And now, looking through God's glasses, let yourself see the faces of the soul mates you've had in your life so far, whether they have been lovers, dear friends, companions, or family members. Look into their eyes and notice love's reflection shimmering back at you.

CHAPTER 2
THE FLOWER OF THE SELF:
INNER CORE TO OUTER PETALS

I wish I could show you when you are lonely or in
darkness the astonishing light of your own being.
–HAFIZ

To love another you must first love yourself.

This simple truth has been stated in many ways and by many wise men and women throughout the ages. In a fascinating world that so easily draws our attention outward, it has long been offered as a lantern to light the pathway back to ourselves. Rather than a moral directive, it is a statement of deep optimism and hope, confirmation that we do have what it takes to love. Just as surely as we are made of oxygen, carbon, hydrogen, and nitrogen, we are made of empathy, compassion, generosity, strength, humor, beauty, and truth. Not only are we capable of loving, we *are* love. So then, perhaps loving ourselves is the inevitable act of an awakened heart, when we recognize and claim our true nature.

Just as the oak grows into its abounding fullness from a single tiny seed that patiently waits within the acorn shell, love too grows outward from the unique soul seed at the center of every human being. When traveling in Belize, Cyndi heard this concept explained in a beautiful way through a story shared by one of the last Belizean medicine men. Through a translator, the elder explained self-love in a different way than Cyndi had heard before, one that she summarizes this way:

First you take the seed and you plant it in the ground, for in the seed is its promise. It will grow to bear fruit for the children and leaves for roofs and bark for healing. **Unless you believe in the power of that seed, however, you will not plant it.** *You will not water it or protect it from the sun. You will not guard it against predators and perhaps you won't even pick the seed from the fruit, leaving it instead for the birds, which will never plant it, for their nature is not to farm, it is to destroy. No, it is up to you to plant the seed that you are. This way, you can become the tree that you can be.*

One of the ways that self-love is expressed is by believing in your inherent power, beauty, and goodness, *even when tangible evidence seems scarce or hasn't yet appeared.* Moment by moment, you can protect and nourish your ever-emerging self through the quality of the choices you make, the thoughts you think, the words you speak, and the actions you take.

Togetherness, too, starts within. It begins with believing in the seed of self that holds the promise of *you*—the wholeness comprised of who you have been, who you are now, and who you are becoming. It's also an invitation to gather and safely welcome back to the home within your heart any parts of yourself that you may have temporarily lost touch with.

This is possible for every one of us. The simple invitation to "just accept yourself" is the start of a great journey. It's the process of looking for, noticing, and gladly receiving the many aspects of ourselves, like so many petals of one exquisitely beautiful flower. As we grow and evolve, self-love empowers us to look through lenses of compassionate honesty rather than harsh self-judgment when examining our lives and relationships.

Traveling through the terrain of this book, you are invited to take this approach; to look through field glasses of kindness and self-respect, especially when you encounter an old wound, a fear, or anything else that might be standing in the way of allowing yourself to fully love.

The Aloneness in Togetherness

The seed of the self, by design, stands alone. To be alone sometimes is not only a good thing, it is a necessary thing. Aloneness is a profound and defining part of the human experience. Let us explain.

The ego (which we will discuss in greater detail in chapter 5) only knows itself as separate. However, the self isn't the solitary structure that the ego imagines. In truth, the self is a melding of many internal traits and states of consciousness, countless inner and outer experiences, and a lifetime of relationships with others. The one "self" is a compilation of the "many."

Whether single or part of a couple, the true meaning of being "alone" is "all" and "one" at the same time.

In the same way, togetherness starts as an experience of being "together" within ourselves even when alone. It's a closeness and tenderness that starts within and extends outward to those around us. Togetherness is like a Mobius strip, a ribbon of affinity and affection that caresses many as it folds back into itself. We intertwine and interweave with others in a myriad of ways, whether we are partnered; bonded with friends; living with parents or children; or sitting in a cubicle at work surrounded by other cubicle people. To connect with our inner selves is to invite connecting relationships—and vice versa. As Martin Buber says, life is an "I-Thou" experience, where "oneness" is discovered in connection with another. "You" and "me"; "them" and "us"; "I" and "we"—together we travel along the path of love and transformation: this is togetherness.

The quality of togetherness that we, your authors, are passionate about cultivating is one that creates connections with *all* the people in our lives, starting with ourselves.

The Separateness in Togetherness

Couples that endure and flourish are those who welcome separateness. Lacking individuality, partnerships can become stagnant and fail to grow and blossom. Enmeshment, an unhealthy entanglement, often makes at least one of the partners feel suffocated. In order to feel like they can breathe, they pull away. In pulling away, the other feels abandoned—and the knee-jerk instinct to grab on even tighter is triggered. This is an age-old pattern that many of us know well. Creating good feelings about the time spent together *and* apart is a dance that we can learn, discovering how to come toward and move away; how to feel our own inner groove while also staying in step and time with each other.

Some of us find ourselves out on the dance floor alone. We're either single or stuck in a relationship that is so disconnected (or even harmful) that we have little choice but to work only on ourselves. In either situation, the steps toward love are the same as they are in a close and committed partnership. In this stage, instead of focusing on the unavailable or missing partner, there is the rich opportunity to create togetherness with ourselves, friends, family, and other members of our love community.

Whether single or in a committed relationship, the truth is that if we don't work on ourselves, we run the risk of becoming needy, resentful, and unable to receive the deepest gifts that relationship has to offer. No matter where we find ourselves on the map of relationships, self-love is our "magnetic north" on the compass; the reference point meant to guide us. You see, even when we are alone, we are not. There are as many "us'es" inside of ourselves as there are people surrounding us. In a sense, we are a community unto ourselves, and love invites us to care as deeply for these "inner selves" as it does for the loved ones who stand outside of us.

44

In Search of the Forgotten Self

Through our external relationships, we come to understand and harmonize the diverse aspects of our internal selves. The same healing and bonding that we can experience with our loved ones applies to the relationship we have with our inner selves. When we embrace who we are internally, we naturally reflect the glow of self-acceptance externally.

How we view ourselves is directly related to how we view the world and other people. We look through the same filters at *everything*. What we have discovered through working with our clients over many years, as well as through our personal experiences in relationship, is the importance of self-knowledge. To "know thyself" with increasing awareness, understanding, and acceptance is the foundation for building relationships that heal, uplift, and endure. That is why, no matter how much therapeutic work or spiritual exploration one has already done, going in search of the wounded self is always a worthwhile journey. We might be called to discover long-forgotten parts of ourselves. We might be summoned from within to see the aspects of ourselves that we thought we knew well with fresh eyes. In either case, as we encounter them with curiosity and compassion, we become more whole in the process. As we take greater responsibility for our emotional well-being, we become more adept at loving.

In the quest for emotional freedom, we can begin to unravel the confusion and misinterpretations we've accrued over the years. To love ourselves is to heal our inner being. One of the most potent paths to doing this is to free the parts of us that are stuck on a treadmill, reliving and rehashing the past. However, this requires the compassionate honesty we referred to earlier. When facing parts of ourselves that we may have forgotten or even rejected, honesty and courage are the best antidotes to the self-judgment that can spring up.

A Conversation with Your Child Self – A Sacred Meditation

The following meditation is a profound yet simple journey for emotional healing and integration. As you read through the narrative, let the flow and feeling of it percolate within you. Once the instructions are imprinted in your awareness, set the book aside and take yourself on this sacred walk into your inner world.

Find a quiet place where you can relax; a warm, comfortable place to sit and have a few uninterrupted minutes with yourself.

Gently close your eyes, and take several slow, deep breaths. Let the activities of the day roll away for the moment. And feel the concerns of the world softly recede, as you turn your attention inward.

As you take another relaxing breath in, imagine taking yourself to a place of great tranquility, beauty, safety, and stillness. This might be a place you've visited in the external world or a place within the beautiful realm of your imagination.

As you arrive in your place of serenity, notice what's happening there—the particular sounds, the fragrances and aromas, the temperature of the air, the quality of light. Really feel yourself being there, enjoying the feeling of safety and peace.

Now, way off in the distance, you notice the figure of a person. It's too far away to know who it is, but you can see that they're walking toward you. Watch them getting close and closer.

As their face becomes clearer, you see that it's a child. It is the little girl, or the little boy, that was you.

At a certain point, they stop, awaiting a signal from you. Invite them to come closer. And closer still. Invite them to come and sit with you in a comfortable place. Let them know that you're eager to talk with them. Sitting together, ask this little one to tell you what life is like for them. As they talk (and move about, squirm, or do other kid-like things), just be there with them, listening with great love and compassion. Allow them to take their time.

Once they've said what they want to say, let the child know that you've heard everything. Let them know that they are going to be all right. Assure them that through the years, you have learned, you have grown, you've made it through. Everything is going to be okay in their future. And they are safe now.

Open your arms to this child, holding and loving them. Let them melt into your loving embrace. Ask them if there is anything else they want you to know about their life and their world. Be a loving parent by staying present, truthful, and reassuring.

When you're both ready to leave, allow this priceless child to magically fit into your heart—where you can bring them with you. Assure them that you'll be there for them from now on; you'll care for them and check in with them on an ongoing basis.

Before opening your eyes again to the outer world, take another soft, deep breath. Notice any feelings and sensations that linger from your time spent together with your child self.

When you feel complete, just open your eyes and come back to the room where you're sitting.

Take a few minutes to write down in your journal or a notebook anything you would like to refer back to later. And acknowledge yourself for tending to your inner world with vulnerability, trust, and love.

The healing that you've set in motion by paying attention to this very real and essential part of you is likely to ripple through your life in extraordinary ways.

The Gifts of the Wounded Self

The fact that you are reading these pages is a signal from your inner self that you want more. "More what?" you might be asking. More closeness, intimacy, and emotional fulfillment, to start with. Perhaps a desire for a deeper and more satisfying expression of love has been unleashed in your soul. The French writer Anais Nin described this turning point magnificently: "And the day came when the risk to remain tight in a bud was more painful than the risk it took to blossom."

Perhaps the flower of *you* is ready to be seen in its full glory. Claiming the many petals of your "self" will lead to the full blossoming of love in your life.

Each of us is comprised of a multiplicity of "selves." There is the Andy who loves to golf, and the Andy who likes movies; the Cyndi who loves classical music, and the Cyndi who prefers the sound of crickets singing. There are aspects of self that are open and eager to grow, and aspects that are so scared and ashamed, they often sabotage our own—and sometimes others'— peace, prosperity, health, and success. These are the "walking wounded within"—the parts of ourselves that are still trapped in experiences that caused physical, emotional, mental, or spiritual trauma. Until they are gently and compassionately released, they will remain locked into the age and maturity level they were when injured. They are not bad or inferior or undeserving. Rather, they are undeveloped aspects of self and soul that were never provided the opportunity to grow and mature. Quite literally, we might have a two-, eight-, or twelve-year-old running our lives—and our relationships.

From a therapeutic standpoint, these underdeveloped aspects of self create discord and problems, including addictions, relationship conflict, and even health challenges, because they aren't content to remain imprisoned—nor should they be. Who wants to spend their life behind bars? This is a crucial point to consider, because so much of the pain that we see in our clients comes from looking only at the problem and missing out on the power of the messages that are being conveyed from within, like emails marked "urgent" by parts of us that were left emotionally bereft in the past.

There is a wisdom built into the *repetitive* nature of our issues. They will not stop knocking at the door until we pay attention. The hurt, disempowered, and sometimes enraged aspects of our child and adolescent selves will not "quiet down and be good" until we take them in our arms, until we listen to them with our whole hearts. If we insist on ignoring them, they hijack important areas of our adult lives. Our ignoring becomes a kind of "allowing" as we sit back and watch the *coup d'état* taking place…repeatedly. It's like Groundhog Day, over and over and over.

It would be an understatement to say that life, especially our relational life, doesn't work well when run by a hurt, outraged, and suffering inner child.

From a spiritual point-of-view, these "wounded selves" are vital and necessary contributors to our existence. Each holds an amazing gift, a perspective, ability, or possibility that has been locked away. For instance, one of the wounded aspects of Cyndi's inner child is a precocious four-year-old, who loves to talk and tell the truth. This part of her was judged and ridiculed when she was growing up. When allowed to lead, the four-year-old gets her in all sorts of trouble. Honesty is great, but it can cut and burn when not padded with kindness. She has learned to consult this brilliant child, consider its intuitive perspectives, and then wrap the resulting insights in intelligent, caring language for self and others.

From a metaphysical point-of-view, the trapped and fragmented aspects are often parts of our soul that have been injured. Cyndi's work postulates that we have lived before and carry fears, damage, defenses, and misperceptions from one life to another. We therefore enter life with issues to heal that reflect these karmic or past-life challenges. Her work often includes returning people to earlier states of being, including the states in-between lives, in order to repair soul fractures and allow integration to take place.

No matter where or how our wounds originated, as we approach life with greater vulnerability and receptivity, we can experience more of the sweetness and fullness that life offers at every turn. We can free ourselves from the emotional constriction and confinement we may have struggled with for years.

Explaining this idea to a client recently, Andy used the story of Guinevere, the queen consort of King Arthur. Guinevere had always been a good girl and did what she was told. She even went along with an arranged marriage. However, there was a passionate side of her that wasn't being expressed. She finally broke out of her "imprisonment" by taking Sir Lancelot as her lover. If she could have given her passionate self greater expression within her marriage, perhaps she would not have been attracted to Lancelot in the first place. Lancelot became a means to an end, a way out of her confinement. Perhaps her attraction to him was really a symptom of an issue that predated both men. It's a story older than time. Estranged from essential aspects of ourselves, we unconsciously go looking for reflections of them in others—we seek wholeness *through* others.

Programs and Patterns of Belief
At whatever point the wounding events leave their mark on us, the

50

beliefs imprisoning these underdeveloped selves are aptly called programs. As you have no doubt noticed, emotional and relational programs work much like software programs, operating relentlessly and repeatedly, until rewritten. The sets of programs that control our actions are called patterns. By their nature, patterns can be difficult to break. These programs and patterns are an aggregation of the messages, ideas, concepts, labels, and slogans we come to intimately identify with. Unquestioned for decades or even lifetimes, our programs and patterns stand guard at the doors of our perception, rarely allowing in any new information. No wonder we report feeling stuck, stagnant, or depressed!

What Cyndi sometimes sees with her clients are programs that derive from psychic intrusions and even parts of other people or spirits that adhere themselves to us. For instance, if our mother was scared of men because she was abused, our fears about men might actually be her fears that we have incorporated into our own belief structure. Some people end up feeling that it was their own fault that their mother or father didn't love them. The mental program that can get activated creates a felt sense of being unlovable. No matter how much we accomplish, earn, achieve, or give, the inner void left by the deep belief that we are unworthy of love is left unfilled.

Closely related to this is the belief that we don't *deserve* to be loved.

More than a mere program, a belief in unworthiness and not deserving can become our nemesis. But, a nemesis can become an ally; feeling unlovable can become a catalyst for seeking love and togetherness. The suffering of separation can propel us to seek the solace of truth.

Unraveling misinterpretations—especially the devastating misperceptions that we are unlovable, undeserving, and unworthy—is one of the threads that will lead us to the beautiful truth of who we really are. We need to challenge the criticisms we heard and learned about ourselves. We have a tendency to absorb the negative things we were told about ourselves and believe them to be a true denigration of our character.

We have a hard time grasping that someone simply had an issue with a behavior. A comment may start off as criticism of something we did, not who we are. Yet, that comment can grow inside of us like a cancer, filling us with self-loathing. Why do we do this? Usually, it's because we hold a negative opinion of ourselves and the criticism serves to reinforce that opinion. When we view ourselves as basically good, the criticisms don't have the same ability to adhere themselves to our psyches. We can then view others' comments with perspective and compassion.

Sometimes people can be truly mean-spirited and intentionally try to hurt us. In those cases, we need to consider the source. Wounded people tend to wound others. We need to rise above their jaded perspective and not take on their pain. In a strange and sad way, some wounded people find a bit of relief when they can cause other people to suffer.

On the other end of the pendulum swing, Andy has seen children take on their parents' pain in order to help relieve them of their suffering. In psychological terms, this is referred to as "negative interjects." The children do this so their parents will feel better and, hopefully, be more available to actually parent. In fact, he has often seen this in children whose parents were Holocaust survivors.

One of Andy's clients is a Rabbi whose father was impossible to please. Whatever the young Rabbi did was never quite good enough for his father. He kept hearing the message that if he were to just try harder, he could do better, and maybe then his father would be pleased. It rarely happened. The message that plagued the Rabbi was, "No matter how hard I try, I will never be good enough." Consequently, every year before the High Holy Days, when he is expected to give several powerful and meaningful sermons, he is stricken with a series of debilitating migraine headaches. Even though he now realizes that his father was unappeasable, he continues to have to challenge that inner voice that tells him he needs to work harder…and even that won't be enough. To date, the Rabbi's headaches are better as they are happening with less frequency and intensity.

The Flower of Yourself

A flower grows and flourishes largely based on the nutrients it receives when it's a seedling. It's somewhat different, however, with human beings. We're a little more resilient. As you're now past the seedling stage in chronological human years, rest assured that there is no need to worry. *It is never too late to flourish.* A flower that wasn't properly nourished in the beginning can be re-potted and tended with loving care at any moment. We can heal from an unhealthy childhood by receiving love and encouragement now. The key element here is in our ability to *take in* the love that is given to us, like a flower opens itself to take in life-giving sun and water.

Sometimes we build walls around our heart in order to protect ourselves from harm. We feel safe behind these walls, but there is no aliveness in "safe." In safe mode, there is very little nourishment allowed in. In this state, we are physically alive but barely scratching the surface of our full emotional capacity.

The builder of these walls is best equipped to take them down, one brick at a time. Through self-love, we are strengthened to begin the dismantling. Loving relationships with others are another way we can break down the walls; sometimes the power of *their* love can turn our resistance and doubt into dust.

The truth is so simple, really. We want to love and be loved. We are wired for love. Einstein's Law of Relativity backs this up. It states that everything in our physical world is only made real by its *relationship* to something else. Through loving and being loved, we create anew throughout our lives.

What are the aspects of yourself that are waiting to be seen, heard, and loved? Before continuing to the next chapter, take a little time to consider this question. Envisioning yourself as a flower (men, stay with us here), what do you see? Are you a rose, a tiger lily, a gerber daisy? As you explore the petals of this flower, what do you see? What qualities and attributes do these petals represent? What are the characteristics of your inner self that long to be free? Take your time for these answers to unfold.

No matter how much inner work you may have already done, these questions are important to explore and to answer. Why? Because there is so much at stake; there is so much pleasure, fulfillment, and love around you. There's a light on the horizon and it is the healing radiance of self-love and self-acceptance. Follow it.

We are about to look straight into the face of that which is at the heart of all the fragmentation, dissociation, and loss of self that we've been discussing. We'll use this warm luminosity to our greatest benefit; to bring light to the darkness that comes from unattended shame and fear.

A Reflective Moment

Think of one aspect of yourself that you have denied, been ashamed of, or kept hidden throughout most of your life; a part of yourself that you have judged as bad or somehow unacceptable. Hold this part of you in your thoughts for a few moments, and simply notice what feelings arise when you observe it with compassion, as a parent consoling a child.

CHAPTER 3
HIDE AND SEEK

Your task is not to seek for love, but merely to seek and find
all barriers within yourself that you have built against it.
−JALAL AD-DIN RUMI

How much do you think the fear of intimacy costs us? How often have you heard people say things like, "I wanted to tell him how I really felt, but I was paralyzed by fear," or "I'm afraid to let love in; I don't know if I could survive getting hurt again"? The next time you overhear people talking about the state of their relationship, or the state of their singlehood, take note of how many fear-based statements are made. It's very illuminating.

And then there are the fears that rarely get verbalized, but we can see evidence of them by a reluctance or an unwillingness to take risks in matters of love.

So many of us let fear guide our lives, dictating some of our most important choices. We become ruled by it; victims of our own vivid and worried imaginations. We may be thoroughly involved in our lives—doing our work, loving our kids, contributing to society—but doing all of that with fear nipping at our heals. We may have a full life yet rarely feel free from anxiety, worry, concern, or even dread. And some of us are flat out paralyzed by fear. It slams the door of opportunity closed at the most inopportune moments, especially when love comes knocking.

For the sake of clarity, we're not talking about the kind of fear that protects us when we're in imminent danger; the undeniably useful fear that says, "Get out now!" when a building catches fire or you spot a mountain lion in your peripheral vision. That's the healthy fear that mobilizes us into action in order to protect ourselves and/or others. We're addressing the fear that runs amok, the fear that turns toxic, poisoning our thought processes and limiting our ability to feel the full range of our emotions. It's the fear that muscles its way into our daily experience, asserting itself into far too many thoughts, conversations, choices, decisions, and actions. And it's the fear that stands in the way of feeling the full depth of joy and peace that togetherness has to offer.

Wherever you are on the spectrum right now—whether fear is an occasional visitor or has taken the reigns of your life—take heart. It's possible to start a new and healthy relationship with fear. After more than three decades of work with individuals and couples around the world, we come to this conversation with certainty: The way to get through fear is to go right at it. Ask yourself, "What's the worst thing that can happen if I face my fear head-on?" Perhaps it would simply be a little embarrassment. It's usually worth the risk and effort to get through to the other side. That is where you will find the freedom to open yourself to others and to be receptive to their love for you. Cultivating a deeper understanding of the link between fear, shame, and the need to feel safe will help you to make the journey.

The Imperative of Emotional Growth

As we explored in the previous chapter, emotions often don't know the passing of time. The hurt, anguish, and fear of a wounded inner child shows up over and over again in our adult lives when that child self is allowed to run the show. This is how we get "stuck" in fear. We become driven by the anxiety, and sometimes panic, of a child that has long been relegated to a psychological construct and not understood to be a vital and real part of who we are.

When we don't uncover and resolve emotions that were especially painful, we can get caught in cycles of repeating what we experienced as children. For example, if we were frequently blamed or called stupid during our childhood, there could be the tendency as an adult to blame others and avoid the pointed finger at all cost.

In therapy sessions with couples, Andy sometimes sees how people are afraid to emotionally show their deepest feelings during the session, which is an indication of how they're functioning together outside the therapy room. One or both people are afraid that if they reveal their honest thoughts and feelings, their partner will reject them. They hide behind a defensive posture of complaints and blame, such as those related to money, sex, or the division of labor. "I have so much on my plate. I can hardly get the bills paid and take care of the kids, let alone figure out how to make this relationship work." Sometimes it's a false sense of bravado. "I'm only doing this for her. I don't really see why we need this." Or even the classic complaint, "Why don't you ever take the garbage out? Do I have to do everything around here?" These are symptoms of common problems. Going deeper with people reveals the real truth, which often involves some combination of fear, sadness, shame, or guilt.

In the quest for emotional freedom, it's important to contemplate that blame, guilt, and shame are much more intricate than one might think. Guilt can sound relatively harmless, until you realize that it is actually anger turned inward. Blame is the projection of shame onto another. The unconscious idea is, "If I can blame you then I can be shameless. I'm not wrong, you are. I didn't do anything bad, you did."

A half-hearted attempt at addressing a rift in the relationship often occurs when one of the partners, deep down, doesn't like him or herself. They believe that since they see themselves as a failure, their partner also sees them as a failure. Again, how we see ourselves colors everything. It reflects how we *think* others see us.

One of Andy's clients had struggled for years with seeing herself as a failure in spite of the fact that she had a loving husband and held a prominent position in a respected company. Reflecting on her childhood and adolescence, she realized that she had always tried to make her mother happy and was unable to do so. Regardless of good grades, awards, or winning behavior, she couldn't take away her mother's emotional pain. Since her youth, the unspoken question that hung like a dark cloud over her marriage and her life was, "How could I feel accomplished, happy, or worthy when I have failed at my main job in life?" Once she realized the impossibility of her mission to emotionally rescue her mom, she began to evaluate her life more realistically and gradually let go of the pattern. Nourished by the realization of her inherent worth—not based on any outward achievements—the roots of her self-esteem deepened and her petals opened to expose more of the beautiful flower that she truly was.

Cyndi approaches her own self-discovery and healing with the same gusto that she brings to her work with her clients. Having been a therapy client herself since she was 20 years old, she meets her challenges with a determination to learn. "What is the most positive thing I can glean from this?" is one of her guiding questions. One day in a therapy session, a life-changing moment occurred that has served to fortify this determination. Working with a therapist who was aware of the abuse that she had endured as a child, the counselor offered a nearly astonishing observation:

"You have grown to distrust your inner child; seriously questioning her memories and the conclusions that she arrived at. But have you ever considered that your inner child was actually right? Have you considered that she was right to think that the behavior of some of the adults surrounding her was crazy?"

This was a profoundly validating realization for Cyndi that deepened her ability to appreciate and listen to her inner child's gift for detecting when something is askew.

For each of us, to heal the wounds of the past, it's essential that we allow ourselves to evolve emotionally and psychologically. Asking questions such as "Can I mature the perceptions that I've held of my past? Can I mature the fear that I've held rather than stay stuck in it?" is a deceptively simple way to invite transformation.

To "mature" the fear and to be free of its hold, there is nothing as potent as understanding our fear. What is the source of our fear? Like an oil leak that springs from the sea floor, churning out unfathomable amounts of sludge, where is all of this fear really coming from? And what will it take to plug up the geyser-like hole that sprung the fear-leak? Answering these questions in full would require an entire book dedicated solely to their intricate layers. Instead, we're going to keep our eye on the mark: supporting you to open your heart to a depth of love that transforms your life. Therefore, our invitation is to come along with us on a quick day-trip, if you will. We're going to hike into the forest of fear to encounter the shame that is so closely tied to it.

The Catalysts of Fear and Shame

Fear and shame. Somehow, we know instinctively that they are inextricably linked. It would seem inadequate to label them as feelings alone; states of consciousness is a more fitting term, just like in Traditional Chinese Medicine where a reference to "Kidney" means much more than two small but hard-working organs responsible for keeping the blood clean and chemically balanced. Instead, it refers to an elaborate bio-system that starts with the kidneys, travels along specific energetic pathways, links to strategic acupuncture points, and impacts every other part of the body. Likewise, shame and fear are complex components of our human make-up. Although we spend an inordinate amount of time battling with them (when they have "gone rogue" on us out of neglect), they are meant to serve us. Both are meant to put us in action—to course correct, to seek healing, to reach higher. When we experience them in a healthy way, they motivate and *move* us. Faced with a dangerous situation, we're moved to run, to rise up, to shout for help. Faced with our vulnerabilities, limitations, and the humbling fact that in some fundamental ways we need each other, we're moved to ask for help, to admit our mistakes, and open ourselves to others.

Then the plot thickens. It was probably hard to find emotionally healthy and integrated role models as children. Equally sparse? Guidance for how to successfully navigate our way through life. In most cases, our beloved mothers, fathers, siblings, and extended families were also left to figure it out for themselves. Rather than being *moved into action* by healthy fear and shame, we get stopped in our tracks. Like a deer in the headlights, we freeze.

Often, this isn't visible to the untrained eye. Many shamed-based people look like they have quite a bit of freedom. But deep within, they are confounded, bewildered by a pervasive sense of being flawed and defective—no matter what they do to "fix" themselves. As we'll soon see, there is nothing to fix.

Ashamed of Being

What are we so ashamed of? We're ashamed of mistakes that we made, things we did that ended up hurting someone, words we can't take back, love we expected but didn't receive, situations that we allowed to continue, and ways that we haven't lived up to our full potential. We're ashamed of things we failed at doing when we tried, and sometimes we're ashamed of failing to even try. We're ashamed of certain thoughts, feelings, needs, and desires. And most wrenching of all is how many of us are ashamed of who we are.

We're ashamed of our humanity. Disconnected from our true spiritual

61

nature, we lose touch with our innocence and the beauty of our *being-ness*. When shame turns toxic, we believe that who we are on the inside is flawed. We go in search outside ourselves to find our value and self-worth. To say that this wears us down would be putting it mildly.

Some of us aren't only wounded by shame; we *become* shame. The more we repress our pain, anger, rage, hurt, and grief, the more we fuel the belief that there is something permanently wrong with us. One of Cyndi's clients recalled an essay that she wrote for a class when she was just ten years old that articulated how shame fed her sense of alienation from others: "All the other children have bright, shiny faces. Mine is green. I am different. I push buckets full of rage deep into the well of my being."

Pushing down the shame and covering it up becomes a way life. It's the nature of the beast. It's like the Whack-A-Mole game where the faster you whack the moles that poke up through the holes, the quicker they keep coming. Whack, whack, whack! Some of us whack down our imperfection with perfectionism. Some of us slap down our fear of failure with a feverish attempt to achieve. And some of us try to squash the certainty that we'll never be good enough by trying to *do* good enough.

Shame as Criticism and Disapproval

Of course, it doesn't stay with us alone. We project our shame and fear onto those closest to us. One of the most destructive forces in a relationship is criticism. When it becomes a chronic way of looking at and communicating with our partner, criticism can be seen as shame turned outward. Whether it's meant as "constructive" criticism or half-kidding, if the receiver takes it as disapproval of their character, the result is not good for either partner. The backlash often causes the couple to disconnect, leading to those moments when the air in the room is thick with tension.

Sometimes criticism is perceived when it's not actually intended. Andy worked with a man who would occasionally push the hair off his wife's forehead. She took this gesture as her husband not liking the way she looked. The truth was that he loved the way she looked and his gesture was a form of affection. When he was a child, his mother would stroke his hair when she was proud of him. However, in his wife's world, her mother would only touch her when she was trying to correct something she saw as out of place. As a girl, she interpreted this as a message that something wasn't quite right; her appearance wasn't "good enough." When the couple learned what the gesture meant to each of them, they were drawn closer together through their mutual understanding.

Another couple came to Andy for help because they said they were "feuding all the time." Almost everything they said to each other was going through a filter labeled "I'm being criticized right now." They were both on the defensive and took comments in the worst possible light imaginable. The husband felt that whatever he did was met with disapproval. Nothing he did was ever enough for his wife. If he helped her out by picking up the kids from school one day, she expressed dissatisfaction because she would focus on another day when he didn't pick the kids up.

Instead of appreciating what he did, she would always focus on what he didn't do. This left him feeling exasperated, resentful, and not wanting to help her at all. She was afraid that if she approved of him that he would get the message that all was okay in the relationship and that he would never be motivated to make changes for the better. Instead, she never let him think he was in her good graces. Her anger was quickly ignited by just about everything he did. Instead of trying to work toward a peaceful and positive resolution, they led parallel lives avoiding each other as much as possible. Not surprisingly, this extended to the bedroom as well. By pushing him away, she felt safe that he wouldn't press her to have sex with him.

Criticism and disapproval kept this couple apart. However, the real problem was deeper than the angry dissatisfaction they both expressed. Often, the outwardly expressed problem is actually a cover for the real issue that lies beneath the surface. In this case, as in many others like this one, anger was a mask for fear. Anger is usually easily accessible, whereas fear is … well, scarier. The deeper issue is the fear of intimacy.

Seeking Safety at All Costs

Fear of intimacy. This phrase is bandied about quite a lot in our psychologically savvy world. But what does it really mean? Honestly acknowledging the impact and the cost of this fear is a crucial step toward allowing togetherness. The disapproving wife above believed that if she were to let her guard down and allow herself to be vulnerable, she would be setting herself up to be hurt by her husband. By keeping him at arms length, she could maintain a feeling of being in control and safe. She would rather be distant than vulnerable. In this case, as with many couples, *it feels safer to be in control and alone than to be vulnerable and to feel at risk.* At an early age, she learned that she needed to rely only on herself to be safe. She was born out of wedlock and her abusive mother blamed her for the hard life she had. Her mother told her that she had ruined her life and that she wished she had never been born. Andy's client brought what she learned as a child into the marriage. In order to stay out of harm's way, she learned to be self-sufficient. For her, it was a matter of survival.

Sometimes conflict between couples is subtler and doesn't necessarily strike us as a crisis that requires outside help, like counseling. Gradually, we can become mired in petty grievances. Little irritations and annoyances can take up enough time and energy to effectively distract us from addressing deeper issues. We may survive our childhood wounds by learning coping strategies to keep us safe, but those wounds aren't healed by simply burying them. As all of us know from direct experience, intimate partnerships eventually bring to the surface whatever needs to be acknowledged and released. No matter how mature and high functioning we are as adults, sometimes our survival instincts can take over. It's hard to trust that someone will truly love us when it didn't work earlier in our lives. "If I let this person in, I can't trust that they won't hurt me. After all, if my mother who is supposed to love me didn't, how can I trust anyone will love me? At some point they will also hurt me, and I cannot go though that again."

Unhealthy shame, in its myriad forms, is a way to hide. Each strategy, usually unconscious, is a smoke screen for hiding our perceived shortcomings and vulnerabilities. They are covers for the gnawing belief that we aren't worthy of love—not from him, not from her, not from them, not from God.

We attempt to hide our shame, AND we attempt to hide *behind* our shame. This little two-step becomes a protective dance. We try to "protect" ourselves from further shame, embarrassment, and pain. We protect ourselves by avoiding connections that could potentially hurt us by exposing our vulnerabilities and further shaming us. We can feel safe through avoidance, but there is no aliveness there. When safety is our top priority in life, that is all we get. This is a truth worth repeating: There is no aliveness in safety. Aliveness is snuffed out by the fear we put in charge of being the Activity Director of our lives. *We feel safe in the pattern rather than feeling safe in the connection with others.*

Hiding in shame has long been a part of the human condition. In the book of Genesis, once Adam and Eve encountered their human weaknesses and experienced the anguish of lost innocence, their lives began to unravel. Rather than coming to God for help and healing, they hid in shame and humiliation. They feared being further exposed. Genesis 3:7 gives us a poignant snapshot of this dynamic: *"Then the eyes of both of them were opened, and they knew that they were naked; and they sewed fig leaves together and made themselves coverings."* But it wasn't their mistakes and misbehavior that were the root cause of their greatest pain. It was the perceived separation from self and God that stemmed from a monumental misinterpretation: In their minds, they hadn't *done* something bad and wrong, they *were* bad and wrong.

This is the problem with leaving important interpretations and conclusions in the hands of our wounded egos. What looks like a simple matter of semantics can dramatically alter a life. You see, *making* a mistake allows for reparations and forgiveness. Whereas, *being* a mistake has a hopeless finality to it. This is how healthy shame turns very toxic. Rather than being cracked open to a deeper and more vulnerable experience of love and connection, Adam and Eve disconnected from their divine source. Their eyes had been "opened," but their perceptions were distorted by fear, and they were looking through the lens of despair.

This is the story of a core wound in our collective soul. What does it mean to be cast out of paradise if not the separation from feeling loved and knowing that we are, every one of us, an irreplaceable expression of the Divine?

Abandoned or Bonded?

At a fundamental level, we bear the wounds of abandonment. Although it may not be the thing we think about over our morning toast and coffee, it's a wound that becomes evident in times of relational duress and conflict. We feel abandoned—by a mother, a father, a lover, a friend, our Higher Power. Some of us even feel abandon by our dreams and the hopeful future we once saw for ourselves. This abandonment feels like loss, and even though loss is a natural part of life, many of us are ill-equipped to cope with it.

When shame and fear are carried for too long, they can morph in resignation; we secretly give up on the possibility that we can be profoundly connected to those we love for the rest of our lives *and beyond*.

Andy recalls a client who had fears come up about her boyfriend in relatively innocuous situations. In one session, she admitted to a thought that had been taunting her for days: "My partner is going away for a weekend. Maybe he doesn't love me. Maybe he'll find someone to replace me." Is that a fear you can relate to? Those are the kinds of anxieties that we don't often verbalize, which is why counseling is immensely freeing; it's a place to give voice to our little worries and big terrors. In the context of relationships, jealousy is one of the most distressing offshoots of fear. Distrust and jealously are easily triggered by the fear of abandonment. How could it be otherwise? Believing that we are wholly inadequate, the next "natural" conclusion is that our partner will find someone better than us. Is this fear not one of the biggest obstacles to togetherness known to humankind?

Truth and Relaxation
So what is deeper and truer than all of that pain and suffering? We want to belong, and we want to *rest* in that bond of connection. We want to relax at the deepest level, trusting that we have always been and will always be "together" with our spiritual family.

What will support you to relax and deeply unwind from the past? If it is being reminded that your attempts to hide have also been a valiant effort to protect the excruciatingly beautiful jewel of your inner self, then take a deep breath and know that that is true.

If it is being assured that you are good enough and worthy of great love, then get ready for the exciting chapter ahead. Among other things, we will look together at how your being "enough" isn't about merely being *sufficient*. We will explore how your being "enough" is actually a state of *permanent abundance*. Your soul is rich. And there is nothing in the world that can alter that fundamental truth.

A Reflective Moment

Take a quiet moment to turn your attention toward the part of you that is still wounded by shame. Is that part of you three years old? Ten years old? Fifteen? In your mind's eye, look into the face of this part of you, and let him or her know that the shame is being healed; that they are going to be okay…that all is well.

CHAPTER 4
CLAIMING THE SPACE YOU'RE IN

The privilege of a lifetime is being who you are.
–JOSEPH CAMPBELL

When a relationship ends, we often hear people say things like, "I've been so enmeshed with him that I don't even know who I am anymore." Or, "I'm looking forward to getting back to myself, to finding out what *I* want for a change." We hear similar sentiments from happy couples too: "I think I've met my match, but I don't want to lose myself in the relationship this time." Or, "I'm crazy about her, but I'm afraid we're spending too much time together."

It seems that men and women have long been perplexed by one seemingly simple concern: How to be with the "other" while remaining rooted in the "self." How to care for another while not neglecting ourselves; how to please without placating; how to be strong without being stringent; how to self-protect without shutting down—these are just a few of the considerations that make up the puzzle pieces that we use to put our lives together.

Too often, the landscape of intimate relationships feels like treacherous territory, where the "self" feels like an endangered species. The path to togetherness gets dotted with landmines that appear as painfully compromising choices—either/or; you/me; all-or-nothing. Remember the precious seed of the self—our core self? When did it get pulled from the ground that nourishes and supports its growth and seemingly thrown to the wolves?

To a large extent, the answers can be found in those defining moments that can only be called "wounding." As we examined in the first part of the book, we often go for decades letting these wounds dictate the way we inhabit our relationships—how much of our true self we allow ourselves to reveal; how much of the "other" we allow ourselves to truly touch. For many of us, the shame and fear of the past determines how we occupy the present.

In the previous chapter, we explored the ecosystem of shame and fear in depth, the emotional jungle of the child and adolescent who, out of necessity, came to conclusions and made decisions that we get to revise in our adult years. In our attempt to feel safe—in our relationships, in the world, in life—we have inadvertently chosen attitudes and behaviors that decrease our satisfaction with self, as well as the happiness of our relationships. This is why we're inviting you onto a new leg of our journey together. Joining forces, let's establish a new paradigm of safety—of what it means to feel and be safe.

This is not the type of safety that requires deadbolt locks or insurance policies (although those are wonderful inventions). It's a safety that comes from knowing yourself and calling on your connection to the divine, not letting it wither on the vine. More connected to your personal "space"— your physical, emotional, mental, intuitive, and perceptive fields—you will have a more solid launching pad for your soul and spirit to soar. So, no matter where you find yourself in relationship right now, whether single or in a 25-year marriage, now is the time to connect more deeply to *you*, to strengthen the roots that connect you to every meaningful thing in your life.

Dusty old limiting beliefs can be updated or replaced. Entrenched ideas (like "I'll never be enough") can be changed. Your pure longing to be intimately connected to yourself and others will help you to make these life-affirming changes.

Rather than get tossed around by the winds of the past, you can stand solidly in your own life, thriving and rejoicing in the now.

On this next leg of our journey, we'll be outlining an exciting formula for deeply inhabiting your life with greater awareness, clarity, strength, and power. The puzzle of "how to come together with another without losing yourself" will be revealed to be one of the most profound invitations of a lifetime. It's the invitation to come home again, back to your core self—where spirit is made visible.

We promise not to saddle you with rules to "get right," but instead offer useful practices to add to your daily life, as you can. They are practices that will lead you to a deeper acceptance of the things that have happened in your life and an honoring of who you are.

The Beauty of Boundaries

What defines the space you know as your own?

An exploration of where you are planted in the garden of your life and how deeply your roots go begins with a look at boundaries.

Traditionally, personal boundaries are seen as our individual limits, the emotional, physical, and behavioral lines that we draw (consciously and unconsciously) to protect and orient ourselves. In relationships of all kinds, boundaries create a structure, an organizing framework wherein we relate to and interact with each other. Boundaries also provide a structure for our own identities, giving us a frame of reference for who we know ourselves to be. These invisible parameters help us to define ourselves by identifying and proclaiming what we believe, value, and want. Whatever their condition may be, whether strong and clear or flimsy and murky, it is our boundaries that dictate what we do, what we allow, and who we choose to be involved with. In this sense, boundaries are the mental constructs that help us to decide what to keep *out* and what to let *in*.

At the subtler levels, our boundaries go beyond cognition to the realm of energy. Our energetic boundaries border our spiritual selves and actually promote our true nature. They serve as mechanisms for protection, but are also the means by which we share our deepest selves. We long to express this inner identity, and establishing the correct energetic boundaries helps us do just that. When developed and managed well, they make sure that our real selves—not the ideas, thoughts, and beliefs that aren't us—are in charge of our lives. They transmit information to the external world, telling everyone exactly who we are, what we want, and how they can treat us. In Cyndi's intuitive counseling work, the auric fields and biomagnetic fields are the primary energetic boundaries that she frequently assists people in repairing and clarifying.

We've all experienced these invisible boundaries. If healthy, they promote healthy connections. Have you ever thought about a loved one and felt compelled to call, only to find out that he or she really needed a friend right then? That's an energetic boundary at work. Healthy energetic parameters also alert us to relationship dangers. Think back to the last time you got a "bad feeling" about someone, only to find out you were right in following your instincts to draw back. If our energy boundaries are damaged, however, we can potentially get close to harmful people or, conversely, ignore the intuitive guidance that might further bonding.

When we come together with another person in an intimate partnership, we naturally share many aspects of our lives, such as home, money, activities, interests, families, and friends. We also share our bodies, minds, emotions, dreams, and visions. When our energetic boundaries are healthy and vibrant, they give us a reliable gauge for determining why, when, and how much to share and merge; keeping us strongly connected to the touchstone of ourselves.

When you look at your closest relationships, what does that tell you about the state of your boundaries right now? Some boundaries may be stronger than others. One may need a lot of attention. You'll know by how you feel when you think of them. For example, when it comes to money and how that impacts your primary relationships, do you feel that you have a healthy, clear boundary? Surveying the current condition of your boundaries, and the relationship you have with this dynamic force field, will be useful as you proceed through the chapters ahead.

Default Boundaries

Given the nature of the ego and the drive to maintain an individual identity, we instinctively create boundaries—whether healthy or constricting. When we look closely, most of us discover a variation on the theme—having some boundaries that are pliant and flexible, that allow us to safely play with the border between self and other, and other boundaries that serve as barricades to shield us from change and uncertainty.

When we're consciously learning and growing, we tend to examine our boundaries along the way, discarding the ones that no longer serve us and establishing new ones that support the expression of an evolving self. On the other hand, when we're living "the unexamined life," we create boundaries by default. When we aren't willing to utter the word "no" and risk the outcome, we still find ways to say "no" with our actions. For example, let's say you don't want to visit your parents (or parent) during the holidays but are afraid of the wrath that may be unleashed if you tell them the truth. So instead, you tell them that you have an important project deadline at work that you can't get out of. The made-up story *becomes* the boundary, but one that probably doesn't feel good. We can justify an action by calling it a "white lie."

In Andy's work, he refers to these default boundaries as "exits." Similarly, Cyndi refers to them as avoidance strategies. When we want to avoid a relationship, a situation, or an impending decision, we can find endless ways of "exiting." It's very common that default boundaries are crafted out of inherently benevolent activities taken to the extreme, like working out too much, being the perpetual student, staying intensely busy at work, doing excessive volunteer work, or even meditating. One of Andy's clients used to meditate up to six hours a day in order to avoid certain parts of his life. When we make ourselves unavailable by tying up vast amounts of time in these ways, we're essentially hiding in plain sight.

Of course, default boundaries are frequently created by the substances and behaviors that make very effective barriers, such as drugs, alcohol, cigarettes, caffeine, food, shopping, TV, and time glued to the computer. Ironically, these "boundaries" can easily become the trap of addiction. One of Cyndi's clients was married to a man who smoked marijuana every night as a way to avoid things that weren't working in the marriage and in his own life. His was a boundary that cocooned him in a private world of self-induced numbness and dull pleasure.

Our Big Excuses
In a similar way, we can use excuses as boundaries too. Often, when we're being fueled by fear and aren't willing to take responsibility for decisions that need to be made and feelings that need to be expressed, we will use an excuse as a proxy until we're ready to tell the truth.

For example, there's the woman who won't leave her husband because she's afraid she won't have enough money when the divorce dust settles. There's the man who doesn't file for divorce because he doesn't want to give up a large portion of his assets. Or, there's the couple that says they're staying together (despite the fact that their relationship has deteriorated beyond repair) because they don't want their kids to be hurt by divorce. These are often the stated reasons that cover up the fears of being alone and of uncertainty—fears that runs deep in many of us.

Additionally, these are the kinds of reasons, justifications, and excuses that keep us from being responsible for what we really want and need—excuses that prevent us from living life more fully.

Another common variation on the theme of "excuses as boundaries" is when a couple has a child and suddenly they do everything as a threesome. What started out as a way to bond as a family can become an excuse for not taking care of the bond of the couple whose relationship is the foundation. With boundaries being almost solely defined by their roles as parents, the lovers drift apart. By not updating their boundaries in ways that support the changing tides of their lives—and that protect their togetherness as much as their autonomy—the kids leave home one day and the parents discover that they have little in common.

One of Cyndi's clients had gained 50 pounds in the three years following a violent attempted rape. Understandably, she had padded her body with a protective shield, a physical "keep out" sign. Over ten years later, she was still grappling with the excess weight and came to the realization that it had become her big excuse. She didn't have to deal with the emotional risks involved with being intimate and vulnerable with a man as long as she kept the boundary of her weight firmly in place.

"You Are Here"

In his psychotherapy practice, Andy helps his clients to see how their boundaries can be a means of "locating" themselves in relationship to others and the world, providing a way to orient that is familiar and safe. We come to identify ourselves with the roles that dictate the parameters of our behaviors and seem to "fit" best, like a comfortable pair of shoes or an expensive suit. And each of these roles comes with their own tailored boundaries. Being the nurturer or the people-pleaser comes equipped with boundaries that specifically fit those roles. Being the boss or the guru comes with a different set of boundaries that keep those identities intact.

In our culture, when people think too much of themselves they're considered narcissists, and when they think very little about themselves they're considered selfless (which can be either a spiritual virtue or neurotic self-abandonment, depending on the particulars). Opposite sides of the same coin, both are examples of personality types that can define the boundaries of self that significantly shape our relationships.

The unhealthy expression of selflessness was poignantly exemplified by one of Andy's clients, a man in his sixties who had been raised to be very dependent on his mother and other women in the family. From a tender, young age, he learned to look to them to find his value, worth, and identity—not an easy pattern to break. Throughout most of his adult life he had gravitated toward women who were well-suited for continuing this dynamic. Relationships were a drug for him.

When he began working with Andy, Henry had recently started dating Claire. As he had done with previous women, Henry would spend a great deal of time thinking about and looking forward to their dates. He would be high for a day if Claire smiled at him, but if she frowned at him, he would be depressed for a week. He would look for and locate himself in Claire, rarely occupying his own skin.

For as long as he could remember, Henry had been attracted to women who were hard to please and prone to being emotionally unavailable. At first, Claire also seemed to draw him close to her and then pull away. He tried everything he could to get her to love him; even leaving glasses of ice cold water by her car door on hot summer days. Just as he had experienced with his parents, nothing he did was enough. His entire focus was a futile attempt to attain her love and appreciation. However, everything began to change for the better as he consciously engaged in the work of locating himself within *himself*. The most important step in reclaiming himself has involved taking responsibility for his life in tangible and measurable ways. Where he used to neglect himself while putting all of his focus on the relationship, he now holds clear and firm boundaries that support ongoing self-care. For example, as he maintains his house, focuses on his business, and spends time with friends, he recognizes more clearly each day that the future he wants for himself cannot be found inside that old relational dynamic. Henry's boundaries have become healthier while his life has simultaneously transformed. In fact, he recently refinished his house and took up a sport that he had enjoyed in his youth. And, by the way, he broke up with the woman he could never please.

On the flip side of the selfless person who locates "outside" rather than "inside," there is the narcissist, the one who fills all time and space with a "what's here for me?" attitude. Cyndi once had a client who came to her reporting that everything was completely fine with his marriage but that he just wasn't happy. "I'm just depressed and want to feel like myself again," he told her. Intuitively, Cyndi sensed that he was cheating on his wife. Later, it came to light that he was in fact having affairs with other women and was accustomed to covering lies with more lies. In fact, Cyndi discovered that he had actually given her a false name when he scheduled his session with her. He was genuinely shocked and angry when his wife eventually found out the truth about him and filed for divorce. Rather than feeling remorse for the pain he caused, when confronted by his wife with proof that he had been unfaithful, he denied it. Where Andy's client had too much empathy with his past partners, Cyndi's client had no empathy for his wife at all.

When we're not seated in our own lives, unable to say "yes" and "no" in ways that are true to who we are and what we want, we can find ourselves entrenched in a web of behaviors that take the place of positive boundaries. Being a people-pleaser is one of the most debilitating and destructive identities imaginable, one that by design requires weak boundaries. One of Andy's clients vividly illustrates this dynamic.

Nancy, a young woman who is the granddaughter of a Holocaust survivor, was born into a lineage of women who learned to stay closely bound to one another, not only to feel safe but to also *be* safe. Nancy learned from infancy to "locate" herself inside her mother, over-identifying with her mother and being connected in ways that were all-consuming. She wanted to please her mother and make her happy, but her mother was not able to be pleased. Instead, her mother berated and criticized her, and nothing she did was good enough. For Nancy, occupying and claiming her space as an adult means understanding that she cannot please everyone, even her mother. One of the tangible ways she's putting this understanding into practice is in the process of buying a house. Where she used to be paralyzed from taking action for fear that her mother wouldn't approve, she is now moving forward with the knowledge that it's likely that her mother won't like the house she picks out. In fact, it would be a betrayal of Nancy's inner child's beliefs if her mother *did* approve of the house. However, as an adult whose desire to grow and evolve is stronger than her need to relive the past, Nancy is gradually stepping into the shoes of one who deserves to have her own life; someone who has a right to inhabit the space she is in.

We see it again and again. The selfless adult started out as the child who didn't get to occupy his or her own internal space and was left with the impossible task of finding themselves "out there." As we made a point to say earlier, the inner child is a real and essential part of who we are, not a psychological construct or theory. Knowing this is central to coming home to our core self. The core self includes *all* of who we are, without exception.

There is an analogy that you may be familiar with, one that offers a potent teaching on this topic. On an airplane, the flight crew tells you that in case of an emergency where there's a loss of cabin pressure and the oxygen masks drop down, you have to put on your own mask first. Once you have gotten some oxygen, then you'll be better able to help others. We need to know and honor the balance between the other and the self. And while we shouldn't neglect others, we can't kill ourselves in the process of "helping" them either. A healthy self needs to come first.

Early in his career, Andy used to work very long hours and would often come home feeling irritable and not knowing how to let go of the conversations he had had during the day. He hadn't yet learned how to have the kind of boundaries with his clients that would allow him to be fully present when he was with them without bringing the energy of their emotions home with him. He eventually learned that everyone benefits when he doesn't over-empathize and absorb others' emotions and thoughts, especially the toxic ones. In a similar way, addressing energetic boundaries with her clients several hours each day, Cyndi sees people taking in energy from other people without any knowledge that they're doing this, from co-workers, friends, partners, parents, ex-boyfriends, and even deceased relatives.

Whenever we aren't conscious of our energetic boundaries, we abdicate the seat of our power to a program rooted in the past. However, the dysfunction that has been perpetuated and repeated for eons can come to an end. And sometimes it only takes a few minutes of clear intention to regain our seat.

When we're working with clients whose long-held boundaries aren't serving them well, the "Inner Heart/Outer Heart" visualization is a process that works very effectively.

The outer heart is magnanimous, taking in information in order to understand it; opening itself to a large number of situations, circumstances, and people. *The inner heart* is more selective and discerning, only open to certain people and experiences. We benefit from the wisdom that both hearts bestow on our lives.

When you are seeking understanding and answers from your heart, ask both your outer heart and your inner heart to illuminate the situation. First, imagine that you are surrounded like an egg with God's golden light. Inside this semi-permeable membrane of love, you are free to perceive things without absorbing feelings, attitudes, ideas, and energies that aren't yours. Ask your outer heart to show you or tell you what it wants you to know, and then ask your inner heart to share its perspective with you.

This simple exercise is a powerful practice for experimenting with new boundaries, spiritual boundaries that are well equipped for keeping negativity out and letting oceans of love in.

The Frontier of Kindness

To allow the depth of intimacy that we truly desire, we need to hold what's valuable to us and to our partner in equal weight. That's a fragile balance to maintain, a teeter-totter that can shift very quickly. But as we claim our own lives and honor our own values, we naturally honor the values of others. In doing so, our awareness expands, and we actually increase our capacity to notice what others value.

What they value begins to take on more meaning for us and impacts the choices we make in relationship to them. As we grow in our ability to see that what matters to them is not the enemy of what matters to us, our boundaries change. Eventually, we discover that as crucial as they are to having healthy and successful relationships, there is something even greater than boundaries for helping us to navigate the terrain of intimacy and togetherness, and that is *kindness*.

When our personal boundaries are expressions of the way we honor, respect, and care for ourselves and others, rather than mechanisms for defending ourselves against life, we surely feel and know the difference.

Kindness in Action

Four Practices for Occupying and Claiming the Space You're In

The practices that follow will usher you to the seat of your core self, empowering you to update your personal boundaries and take ownership of your life at a new level of mastery.

---

1. Honoring Yourself

All healthy external relationships start with self-respect and self-love. By strengthening your relationship with yourself, you are able to inhabit your own life more fully. This process starts with taking good care of yourself. To take it a step further, occupying your space means taking good care of yourself in *all* areas, and not at anyone's expense.

What parts of your life are in need of some loving care attention?

One way that Cyndi takes care of herself and honors her own energetic boundaries pertains to the way she handles rushed requests, such as requests for an interview, a phone meeting, or perhaps a piece of writing for one of her publishers. When a request is actually a strong demand, some discomfort can get triggered. What Cyndi has learned is that if she feels any tightness—physically, emotionally, mentally, or energetically— she waits 24 hours before she responds to the request. In other words, if she feels inner conflict, she waits. She says, "When I'm divided within myself, I ask God for a solution that is more encompassing than the ones I'm currently considering."

When you react instantaneously in moments of stress, it's likely that your inner child is calling the shots. But if you let it all sit for a while, you're more apt to respond from your adult self.

Cyndi works with a woman who is nearing 80 years old and learning now how to honor herself. The mother of six children and deeply influenced by her Catholic heritage, she initially didn't want to see Cyndi but was driven to by a gnawing regret for mistakes she believed that she had made when her children were very young. In particular, she had spent years feeling badly about herself for not being able to give enough attention to one of her youngest children when another was in the hospital for an extended period. Cyndi's work with her has been centered on helping her to create new boundaries and discover new ways to occupy the space in and around her so she can feel good about herself. This includes understanding that when people give her their feedback, she doesn't have to respond if she doesn't want to. She's discovering for the first time that although she doesn't have to avoid or block out other people's opinions, she doesn't have to do anything about them either. She gets to choose when to change, when to respond, or who to help. As she practices forgiving herself, old behaviors geared toward trying to make up for the past are subtly falling away. Whether twenty years old or one hundred and twenty, we deserve to be free from the shackles of the past and honor ourselves in the present.

What do you like to do every day?

On a daily basis, find simple ways to honor yourself. Find three things you like doing every day and do them. Cyndi likes to walk, read, and drink ice tea. Andy likes to have lunch with family and friends, take a short afternoon nap, and read the sports page. Whatever you choose, know that you deserve to have pleasure, so let pleasure be your guide. Does it light up you, energize you, calm you, or delight you? Prioritizing pleasure is, without a doubt, one of the most effective ways to claim the space you're in, where, more and more, you embody your life with a smile on your face.

2. Soothing Yourself

Your inner child asks of you this question: "If you live your life the way YOU want to, will *I* survive?" If you're like most people, you usually ignore this part of yourself, while it pulls and tugs at the fabric of your life, demanding your attention. With its vulnerabilities and fears having been dismissed, it is deeply interested in the way you're living your life and wants to be considered with each choice and decision. One of the main characteristics of maturity is being able to respond to these concerns and to soothe yourself, providing relief and comfort for yourself by tending to your emotional needs.

One strong indicator that your inner child is frightened and trembling in a corner is when you're looking at a challenging situation in your life and you are *certain* that you don't have a choice in the matter. You know those times when you feel backed into a corner? You may say things like, "I HAVE to; I don't have any choice." Or, "If I don't do it, nobody will." Or, "If I don't nail this perfectly, I'll get fired." These are the moments when the best thing to do is stop, recognize the feeling of "choiceless-ness," check your assumptions, and acknowledge the needs and desires that you're afraid won't get met.

As a psychotherapist, whenever Andy is asked to define what mental health is, he often says that it is the awareness that you have choices. With practice you will find that cultivating the awareness of choice is profoundly soothing to your soul.

3. Embracing Choice through Self-Determination & Responsibility

In moments when you're feeling clear, awake, and firmly rooted in yourself, you know that you can only be responsible for yourself. Although you care very deeply about the well-being of others, you can't be responsible for their happiness, not even in a marriage or a parent-child relationship. It's just not possible, and trying to accomplish that task results in frustration and pain.

When we attempt to be responsible for others, we invade their right to problem solve, to learn, to heal, and to access their own inner resources. It's the birthright of each one of us to access our own inner resources and to determine the right course of action for ourselves, even if we stumble and fall along the way—which we inevitably do. Becoming self-determining is so fundamental to the dignity and happiness of an individual that helping people to strengthen this internal capacity is one of the primary tenants of therapy.

Cyndi has two children, as does Andy. And despite the natural urge to protect them, they both had to learn that they can't rescue their kids in every difficult situation or protect them in every area. Some parents handicap their kids this way. Children don't learn to be healthy, resourceful, self-referring and self-determining individuals if they aren't allowed to find solutions and come to their own insights and conclusions. Each of us grows as we pick our way out of the debris of our mistakes and struggles, and we have to allow our loved ones to do the same. We can help them to cope and deal with their challenges but not shield them from all of life's weather.

Every time we make a decision, especially the decisions that have significant impact on our relationships, we have an opportunity to determine the course of action that will increase intimacy or chip away at it. "Do I yell and scream right now, or do I take a deep breath and tell him I'm scared? Do I stay here and face the situation, or do I run out the door?" Recognizing that you have control over your own reactions allows you to *choose* how you are going to handle a situation.

One of the big choice points we encounter with our clients is the moment when they're trying to decide what to do about a relationship. While one person may be trying to determine if they should take the commitment deeper, the other may be considering ending the relationship.

Have you ever found yourself struggling for an extended period trying to decide what to do about a relationship? If so, you know it can be an excruciating experience! This type of emotional juncture is the perfect time for practicing kindness. One way to practice kindness is simply to realize that sometimes it takes a long time to leave a relationship. The quick, clean, and decisive break-up is the exception to the rule.

Again, occupying and claiming the space you're in can mean giving yourself some extra breathing room and choosing to NOT make a decision right now... being willing to wait and to find out.

4. Accepting Yourself and Your Life Lessons

As we explored in the last chapter, it is all too common to feel shame about ourselves and our lives, even if the shame is cleverly concealed behind layers of accomplishments and success. This shame can lead us to adopt false boundaries and settle for repetitive patterns of interacting with the people who mean the most to us. It is shame that can take us outside of ourselves, leaving us adrift in a sea of self-doubt, and sometimes self-loathing.

Although we would never suggest that there is one-size-fits-all antidote to healing shame, there is a simple practice that's profoundly effective when applied liberally to inner wounds. The practice is one of self-acceptance. Not the kind of acceptance that is really resignation all dressed up ("Oh well, I can't do anything to change it, so I might as well just accept it"), but the real thing—the acceptance that is a whole-hearted and courageous acknowledgment of who you are and what you have lived.

For many pages now, we have been examining what happens when you look at yourself and your life through the eyes of a wounded child. This process has been for the purpose of cultivating a heightened awareness of yourself and engendering self-compassion. It has also been an opportunity to view your life through your emotionally mature eyes, to see the fullness and rightness of everything you have lived.

If you feel stuck and are having trouble seeing what is right about your biggest challenges (and by "right" we mean that they have caused you to learn, grow, and evolve), one practice that can help you to have a shift in perception is to approach the challenge or lesson as a prayer, asking for divine support to get the gold from it: "What is my lesson here? How has this challenge been a way for my soul to grow?"

Having gone through the difficulty of divorce, Cyndi is clear that she would never trade the lessons she has learned. Being a single mother has allowed her to develop her masculine side, to take charge of paying the bills, to become adept at making the difficult decisions, to become stronger and more resilient. She revels in her life as a single mother who spends an extraordinary amount of time in bleachers watching sports (and fitting in writing deadlines in the moments between cheering with the other parents). In her acceptance of the way her life with her boys has unfolded, she is left with gratitude.

Both Cyndi and Andy remind their clients on a daily basis that self-acceptance is really a recognition of what is deeply true: Not only are you enough, you are more than enough. You are whole and complete. You are full in soul and spirit.

Preparing to Love More Deeply

From this place of fullness, it's now time to step into Part II, into the depths of loving another. With an updated understanding of your boundaries and more fully inhabiting your life, you are ready for more togetherness. You have further tended to the seed of your core self, your deepest inner being that has the capacity to love and be loved. Can you feel that vibrating aliveness right now? This is your divine essence, which has no problem whatsoever loving *everything* that previously caused you anguish, embarrassment, shame, humiliation, fear, or pain. The spirit that shines through your eyes is undaunted. To your core self, it has all been grist for the mill of awakening.

A Reflective Moment

Before moving on to the next page, reflect on your life as a whole right now—in body, mind, and spirit. What is the one thing you need at this time to inhabit or claim your life more fully? Is there a decision to be made? A boundary to be established? An action you can take?

CORNERSTONE II

Togetherness with a Future Partner

THE SECOND CORNERSTONE of togetherness is
focused on the loving relationship you wish to attract.
But there is an important caveat to this cornerstone:
Your "future partner" can actually be the person you're
with right now! Each of us are growing and evolving.
The person you will be tomorrow is not the same person
you saw in the mirror this morning. In that sense, your
future partner may be someone you have yet to meet or
the person you've been loving for the past 30 years. In
either case, Part II can be an extraordinary catalyst for
making peace with your past relationships (including
past relationship issues) and preparing the ground for a
new depth of intimacy in your life. Upon reading these
three powerhouse chapters, you will have a clearer
understanding of the push-pull dynamic that happens in
relationships; greater insight regarding your expectations,
desires, and dreams for your relationship; and renewed
gratitude for the experiences you have had and the people
you've loved. All the while, you will be setting the stage for
relationship magic in the future.

CHAPTER 5
SEPARATE AND CONNECTED

"No human relation gives one possession in another—every two souls are absolutely different. In friendship or in love, the two side by side raise hands together to find what one cannot reach alone."
—KHALIL GIBRAN

You know the feeling when you first fall in love? When there's a warm glow of possibility around virtually everything? The promise of romance and deep belonging is in the air…and it's blissfully intoxicating.

When we first enter into a relationship, often called the stage of infatuation, we are filled with tingling excitement and expectation. Although loathe to admit it, many of us dream of a life like Snow White had with Prince Charming. The minute Prince Charming wakes Snow White from her long sleep with a deep kiss, their love is instant. *Voila!* They are both rescued from the perils of ordinary life by love's enchantment. Of course you remember how the story ends: They ride off into the sunset together, presumably to live a life of eternal bliss. We never see what happens in the months and years to come. We're left with assumptions that underlie some of our secret yearnings, like how it might really be possible to wake up each day like a magical prince or princess, being held tenderly in the arms of the partner of our dreams.

Beginnings *are* blissful, sometimes even rapturous. It's understandable that we desire a lifetime of feeling the way we did in the beginning. We finally met our soul mate, the one who will give us the love we have always desired. At least that's what our child and adolescent selves are hoping for. We want to feel connected; we want to merge, like a matching lock and key that were designed only for each other.

When that blissful love doesn't remain—and it never does—we feel let down. The heights we feel in the beginning eventually become fewer and farther between, and we're left wondering if there is something wrong with the relationship or, even worse, with *us*.

One of the primary reasons that relationships break apart is because of the unrealistic expectations we place on the relationship and on our partner. Although we may not be fully aware of it, at a certain level of consciousness we expect our partner to continue to be just like us.

Finding Out That We Are Different

In the beginning of a relationship, we can hardly believe how compatible we are. We tell our friends: "We are so similar. We like the same movies, restaurants, books, and vacation spots. It's uncanny!"

At first, we think being compatible means being the same.

In the beginning, it's also common to think that our new partner truly *knows* us, endowing them with a level of empathy they may or may not have. We feel so lucky that someone so wonderful cares about us and seems to know us so well.

As we spend more time together, we start to notice something that can be very unsettling. We begin to notice how *different* we are from one another. This sobering awareness can make us feel uneasy, and we may start to lose our balance in the relationship. The differences between us can start to rub us the wrong way. We may see our partner as either inattentive or too attentive. We may see them as overly committed to their personal development and growth or even self-obsessed. We may even blame them for changing the way we feel about them. We think, "If he knows me, why would he treat me this way? I wouldn't do this to him." These are telltale signs that the infatuation stage is fading. When we start thinking, "I wouldn't do this to them," the emphasis is shifting to how we're different from each other, and we don't like it. We want our partner to think like us because, if they did, they would know exactly how we want to be treated. If they loved us, they would know just what we want, when we want it, and would always give it to us. Also, we realize that we are not the only person or thing our partner cares about.

Let us all admit that there have been times in relationships when we have wished and wanted to believe that our partner might be exceptionally intuitive, even a mind reader. The truth is that when we are not seen, heard, and understood, we may feel separate and alone.

"Look, I'm just like you!"

At various times when we were children, we worked hard to avoid feeling separate and alone, being on the outside looking in. We adapted to our parents' framework. Like little sponges, we soaked up their ideas, beliefs, attitudes, and ways of expressing themselves. Driven by the innate need to belong, to feel safe, and to be loved, we contorted ourselves to be like them and to fit in, which made sense to us when we were young. Being "the same" is like a silent mantra in many family systems. Our parents painted a picture of what was "real" and, as children, we tended to copy it. Often, parents proudly begin to "claim" their children when they are young by saying things like "you're just like me." While this helps children build their self-image, it can also send the message that "you should act just like me."

As commonplace and understandable as this is, the cost of trying to be "just like them" was (and is) very high. Sometimes we felt shame for being different from what our family system prescribed. But there was an even more painful fissure. When faced with the shame and the fear of alienation that often resulted from acting in ways that were different from them, we created an "adaptive self" as an attempt to comply—even if it meant going against our true sense of who we were.

Breaking free, discovering our individuality, and healing shame along the way, is one of our great life quests. Separating from familial expectations is an essential part of the process. When Andy was a young man, he was expected to become a businessman. At one pivotal point, the owner of a lighting store was going to retire and sell Andy his business, which would have been a dream come true for someone else. The man was basically going to hand the thriving retail outlet to Andy on a silver platter. However, to Andy this was an unimaginable fate. He knew his destiny didn't involve being a storeowner, and he never even made it to the interview.

A Separate Point of View

In their aspirations for Andy to be the owner of a business—a traditional and respectable vocation—his parents were looking through their own lenses of perception. Out of their love for him, they wanted him to have stability and predictability. Of course, each of us is looking through the only set of eyes we have—our own. Swimming along in a continuous stream of our particular thoughts, feelings, and perceptions, it's quite easy to make assumptions about what is real and true for other people too. Often it's the drive to find our commonalities and to be the same that fuels these assumptions.

Author Peter Russell referred to our conflict about individuating when he wrote about our "skin encapsulated egos"—a construct of separateness that we spend years trying to both protect and break free of. It's the ultimate "push-pull" relationship. We want to be the same, yet we want to be different. We want to be separate, and we want to be connected. Most people spend a lifetime feeling various levels of conflict around this psychological paradox.

Seeking Commonalities to Shield Us from Death

We know that our family histories profoundly influence how connected or separate we feel in relationship to others. We know that our life experiences influence and shape the boundaries that invisibly separate us from everything that we see as "not us." But there is an even deeper influence, the primordial basis of the "push-pull" relationship that the ego has with reality.

In the normal developmental process, we all develop what Freud called the Ego—the built-in human mechanism that establishes our individuality while trying at the same time to stay connected. Your ego. Our egos. They are all constructed the same way. Although breathtaking in its usefulness as it helps to inform us along the journey of life (like a GPS that alerts us to a right turn up ahead), we have mistaken our ego for having an ability and capacity that it just does not have. The ego is the psychic apparatus that allows us to experience and interact with the outside world, our personality. And as it equips us with an individual identity, a "self" that we wish to preserve and protect, the ego becomes a sort of survival mechanism. The ego struggles with being separate without being abandoned or annihilated by the "other."

Looking through the eyes of our egos, we feel separate. When we feel separate, we feel too alone. On the metaphysical level, when we feel too alone, we experience the fear of non-existence, or death.

Cyndi has written extensively about death and dying in some of her earlier books, shedding meaningful light on this mystery that is central to all of our lives. One of the distinctions she makes goes beyond the fear of death and into the fear of "not existing." This desolate fear is one the scariest concepts that we contend with as human beings. And 99.99% of us grew up in a culture where everyone else was trying to escape this elemental fear, too.

Seeking commonalities with our partner gives us great comfort that momentarily protects us from the fear of non-existence, or death.

It makes sense that we would be threatened by our differences. A frightened ego will go to great lengths to reconnect and find commonalities. The boundaries that we explored in the previous chapter are often shaped by this drive for consolidation with others. We capitulate, placate, fabricate, and otherwise give up our core self in order to ensure this protection. If we dig even deeper, we can see that even the fear of not being needed in relationship is another layer of this existential fear. "If you need me, then I exist. I am real." On the other hand, we can lose our individuality and anxiously fear annihilation by being fully enmeshed with the "other."

At first glance, addressing the topic of death would not be considered a very sexy or exciting conversation as it relates to intimacy in relationships. It certainly isn't the primary message being delivered in most relationship workshops or books on the subject. But this is where we wish to step outside the norm and offer you a message that you may find profoundly comforting, refreshing, and enlivening as you proceed with us on this journey of togetherness.

Understanding that death is the natural culmination of life is both real and unreal. We are aware that all people die, yet psychologically, the fear of death can be a misinterpretation of the feelings of separation. The reality of death does not have to steal the freedom, joy, and light that are your birthright. Although it can serve to attune you to the exquisite preciousness of each breath, it was never meant to be the stealer of dreams, intimacy, and togetherness.

We all need to learn to soothe ourselves around unwarranted worries we hold about death, no matter how long we've held them. We invite you to consider that birth and death may be one and the same; both births into a new realism of being. Contemplate the possibility that life, love, and you are untouchable, all existing outside of the polarity of birth and death. Right now, you can wrap your ego in a wonderful security blanket made of your own deep knowing—there really is no death, not in the way that we have imagined it. Self-soothing involves the ego integrating the reality of death into our consciousness rather than reacting to the paralyzing free-floating anxieties of death. In other words, all is well and you are safe to explore the bounds of separateness and connectedness for all of the fulfillment and adventure they will bring.

The End is Only the Beginning

The journey of cultivating and experiencing togetherness involves reorienting ourselves; discovering that what we have feared as endings are, in truth, new beginnings. When we first experience the bliss of togetherness with a beloved, there is a sublime sweetness in discovering what we have in common. But when the initial infatuation stage ends the sweetness need not go sour.

Rather than throw in the towel ("I *knew* it was too good to be true. I was just waiting for reality to set in.") or dig our heels into the ground of the way things were ("What can I do to hold on to the magic?"), we can approach our relationships with emotional maturity, understanding that they don't continue on as they started. They are ever-evolving. When the infatuation stage ends, the real relationship can begin. This is when an emotional and spiritual depth that is lasting and meaningful can take root. By taking the relationship past the stage of infatuation, we sacrifice great heights for great depth. As the newness of a relationship fades, a depth of understanding our partner takes over and can continue to deepen throughout the lifetime of the relationship.

Bridging the Gap of Unevenness

In our Camelot story, Guinevere got tired of being "taken care of" and emotionally and intellectually dismissed. Not being seen, heard, or understood exacerbated her feelings of separation and isolation. By virtue of being Queen during a time of chivalry, she remained subservient to Arthur and without a voice in determining what took place in the kingdom of their life together. *Their relationship never bridged the gap of unevenness.* Arthur remained separate from her as king, and Guinevere remained separate from him as she gave much of herself to the relationship with Lancelot. Although Guinevere and Arthur loved each other, their interests and affections were explored separately. They lived separate lives. Their story is one that is lived by millions of couples today.

Bridging the gap between separateness and connectedness is possible. And there are so many riches available to us when we finally reach each other in the mysterious middle. It turns out that discovering and honoring our differences is actually the spice in relationships! Relationships become thrillingly alive as we learn to accept, appreciate, and even celebrate each other's differences.

When Andy begins working with a couple for the first time, he asks them to start from this premise: *You are not me, and we are both right.*

These words establish a basis of communication that rests in self-responsibility and assures a blame-free zone. They also provide a bridge, one that honors our differences, as well as the boundaries that help us to express our deepest selves. During his studies with Hedy Schleifer, the renowned psychotherapist and relationship coach, Andy learned to instruct couples to metaphorically "cross a bridge" from their world to their partner's world and explore their partner's "neighborhood." This is a wonderful image that invites a warm and welcoming way of viewing the world that the other person inhabits. With an open mind and heart, Hedy asks the listening partner to detach himself or herself from their own worldview and enter their partner's world. In this way, they are able to quiet their own reactive voice and practice being receptive to their partner.

Relationships are intricate. We can enhance many aspects of a relationship by listening with compassion; especially those areas that can be hot spots of conflict, such as sex, money, trust, commitment, and matters of co-parenting. Therefore, listening with compassion means choosing to let our partner's thoughts, feelings, and perceptions matter to us. Compassion asks us to bring heightened awareness of our own filters to the conversation with the other. When we are willing to put our interpretations, biases, and assumptions aside so that we can listen to our partner without judgment, we can then truly get a glimpse of the world that they are experiencing. If you have been on either side of this quality of interaction, then you know it is one of the most bonding and intimacy-producing experiences imaginable.

When we put ourselves in our partner's shoes for a moment, we're able to understand that everyone does "togetherness" differently. Of course, it takes time, often years, to grow into this understanding. Andy started to learn this lesson many years ago, when he met the young woman who became his wife.

Andy met Tess when he was 22 years old, and they were married by the time he was 23. He was from Chicago, and she was from a small town in Iowa. Without much money between them, they bought bicycles for entertainment. One day they were riding bikes together up a hill when Tess fell and got scraped up. Andy instinctively went to help and console her, but she put her hand up to stop him, saying, "Stay away!" So Andy did what any "mature" young man would do and sped away on his bike. That night, when they talked about the incident, Tess told him that she did what people do in a farm town in Iowa: "You take care of yourself," she told him. It was his first moment of realizing how different they were. They've been together now for 39 years. To this day, when Andy is sick, he wants Tess to check on him every ten minutes. When Tess is sick, she wants Andy to check on her the next day. Their love for each other honors and embraces these basic differences. It is interesting that both Andy and Tess, like all couples, have different ways to getting the same needs met.

Each of us is separate and different, but that doesn't equate to being disconnected from one another. We can be separate and still love and be loved. In fact, we connect *through* love, which welcomes our idiosyncrasies rather than being put off by them.

Different Players on the Same Team

Denial is nothing new. Just consider for a moment the stories of Romeo and Juliet, as well as Guinevere and Lancelot: Their love affairs were written in the heavens, but not on earth. In order for closeness and intimacy to last, couples need to have one foot in the heavens and the other grounded on the earth. The heavens are filled with soul and romance and thinking that anything is possible. Having a foot on the ground means to be grounded in reality: "Where will we live? Who will our friends be? And how will we pay the bills?" Romeo and Juliet, Guinevere and Lancelot, all of them would be hard-pressed to answer these earthly questions.

We need to be able to stand in each other's shoes from time to time and allow for a difference of opinion. We already know that we don't see eye-to-eye on every subject, and sometimes we don't see eye-to-eye on some of our most basic values. But these areas of difference can be navigated and negotiated. One of the skills required to work with our differences starts with an understanding that we are on the same team. With the compassionate listening and empathy that we have described, consensus, solutions, and agreements can be found. It's true that it takes some effort and time, but what's the rush? Togetherness is a lifetime adventure.

Even "uncoupled" couples can be on the same team. Cyndi and her ex-husband have been divorced for ten years and, even with their differences, are committed to being the best co-parents possible. Passionate about raising their son in an environment of harmony and peace, they both put one foot in front of the other to find the best ways to bridge the gap—to honor everyone's differences and remain connected for the sake of love of their child. One example relates to how they negotiate the differences between their spiritual paths.

Cyndi's ex is a Pentecostal Christian, while her own approach to faith is more metaphysical, embracing the essential energy that illuminates our lives. With their son, his dad teaches him about the Christian path, and Cyndi teaches him about the ways that we are all the same in spirit. Together, they have found common ground made of mutual respect. They never denigrate one another's beliefs, nor put their son in a position to have to choose between them.

Recently, their son expressed fear about dying and asked both parents for comfort and support. After talking with his dad and getting assurance that he is always held safely in God's loving arms, he then wanted to hear about a near-death experience that Cyndi once had. He had heard the story before and wanted the uplifting assurance that it might provide once again.

After pondering the guidance he had received from both parents, he asked his mom, "Okay, but what if I'm not a good enough Christian?" (There it was again: the "not good enough" thorn in the side of our humanity!) This was an easy gap to bridge for Cyndi, as she said, "A Christian is just somebody who loves, so of course God is going to accept you."

Cyndi and her ex-husband weren't meant to stay together as a married couple, but they are closely bonded as co-parents. They too live the paradox of being separate and connected; honoring their differences and in awe of the mystery that brought them together as a couple in the first place.

Whether we're standing on the same shore or separated by an ocean made of time or misunderstanding, all relationships are catalysts for growth and healing.

Tilling the soil of your awareness and fertilizing the ground of under-standing, you are ready now for the next passage on your journey. In this chapter, our hope is that your empathy has grown as you've explored the relationship between separateness and connection with the people you have loved. In preparation for opening up to more love than you've ever imagined, it's time now to fully embrace even the most difficult relationships you have had. Even if you think you have already gleaned the knowledge that you needed to get and have moved on, we ask that you come with us on another foray into the wilds of relationships—specifically, the difficult relationships you have struggled to figure out, repair, rebuild, or break out of. We're going to show you how the drama that lies beneath them is a portal to awakening.

A Reflective Moment

Think about your closest relationship, whether that is with your spouse, partner, or best friend. Reflecting for a moment on the ever-evolving nature of relationships—and the dance of separateness and togetherness—how has your relationship evolved in ways that have happily surprised you?

CHAPTER 6
MAKING PEACE WITH DIFFICULT RELATIONSHIPS

We seek not rest but transformation.
We are dancing through each other as doorways.
—MARGE PIERCY

Each day of the week, we (Cyndi and Andy) open up our schedule books to review who we will be working with as the day unfolds. Looking at the names of the individuals and couples there on the printed pages (true, some of us still use old-fashioned appointment books), we begin to mentally and energetically prepare for the conversations to come, knowing that people will step into our offices or dial our phone numbers to discuss matters of great importance and meaning in their lives.

What we both know in advance is that 90% of the people we will talk to that day will be addressing relationship concerns—most often intimate relationships with husbands, wives, boyfriends, and girlfriends. And, of course, many will come to address other key relationships—children, parents, siblings, co-workers, employers, business partners, and others. Although the specifics vary greatly, at the heart of the matter is the desire to be free of patterns that limit their ability to experience closeness, fulfillment, contentment, and joy in their relationships.

As for the other 10% of the people we will work with on a given day, it could be said that they too are coming to us with relationship issues—their relationship with themselves, their relationship with life, their relationship with God. Relationship with an "other" is the ground upon which we stand as human beings in a world of duality.

You've most likely heard the word "duality," which is often used to explain the nature of the world. What exactly does this concept mean, especially in relation to relationships? Viewing the world through the ego's field glasses, we don't see the state of oneness that is our true nature, our true home. What we see instead is a dance of opposites, each in relationship to one another—night/day, up/down, in/out, hot/cold, pain/pleasure, love/hate, us/them, you/me.

Alternating between baring our souls and guarding our hearts, relationships beckon us forward, always inviting us to grow and evolve. But quite often, this growth is spurred on by frustration, anger, jealousy, hurt, and sometimes pure, unnamable emotional pain.

We usually enter into new relationships full of hope and excitement, and sometimes we enter into them with a good amount of caution and doubt. When it comes to intimate love relationships, there is hardly a human being alive who hasn't struggled with either a "difficult relationship" that is now in the past, or a difficult pattern within a relationship happening here in the present. Just as a child is basically guaranteed to fall and skin his or her knees and cry tears of embarrassment, as adults we can rest assured that relationship will bring us to our knees once again. In our journey to emotional and spiritual wholeness, we will, at one time or another, feel misunderstood, jealous, betrayed, rejected, hurt, and grief-stricken.

Why do we put ourselves through this? What is so irresistible that we would subject ourselves to so much turmoil? Having a relationship and loving someone is an amazing thing because nearly 100% of the time it ends tragically; either one of the partners dies or one of them leaves.

We take the risk to love and to share our lives, and we're bound to get hurt and hurt the other, consciously or, more frequently, unconsciously. In moments of devastation or emptiness, we may hear ourselves saying, "I just don't think I can go through that ever again." Sitting on one side of the door with any angry and hurt partner on the other side, or looking at a phone that isn't going to ring, it is understandable that we come face-to-face with doubt, distrust, resistance, and cynicism.

So, again, why do we bother? What is so compelling that we muster our courage, over and over again, to be together? Love is.

Love is the magnetic force that draws us steadily together, the "one" drawn to the "other." We are wired to seek intimacy, love, and belonging. Swiss psychologist Carl Jung wrote volumes on how the human psyche strives toward wholeness, always striving to complete itself and to become conscious in the process. Far more than a mental construct, the psyche is the soul itself, moving with unspeakable grace through treacherous terrain on the journey home to a completeness that is beyond comprehension. This is no small feat: seeking individuation in our humanity while seeking oneness in soul and spirit.

In the previous chapters, we have focused on some of the primary ways that relationships make this process of individuation possible. We find our true self in the center point between being separate and yet connected. Becoming an individual, however, isn't the end of the quest. We must now deepen our understanding of ourselves by seeking to understand how we "are" in relationships. A good part of this journey involves exploring our most difficult relationships or relationship patterns, those that we wrestle with when seeking togetherness.

There is a prerequisite to analyzing your relationship hardships. You can't judge yourself. After all, none of us deliberately seek out relationships that will feel like psychological endurance tests. Rather, at the beginning of any relationship, we are filled with great optimism and often dismayed at the other end. We, your authors, want you to hang on to that positive attitude. We are 100% certain that all relationships are catalysts for evolutionary leaps of consciousness. Sometimes the leap happens on the other side of the relationship, after a break up or a death, but that doesn't diminish the power and beauty of the growth that has happened.

When Cyndi is working with clients on their most tenacious and unwelcome relationship patterns, one of the issues that she frequently finds at the center of the storm is a belief that they were never wanted in the first place. Born into a family situation wrought with conflict and strife, they decided that their arrival on the scene was just too much in an already tenuous situation.

As we explored earlier, many of us were hit with waves of shame and fear as we landed on the shore of our lives. And we came to the ravaging conclusion, usually hidden in the shadows of our subconscious minds, that we aren't worthy of the love we want with every cell of our being. Cyndi intimately understands this belief, as she interpreted the painful conflict between her mother and father as confirmation that she wasn't wanted; she believed she was a part of the *cause* of their strife. Happily, she decided early on to embrace every opportunity to unravel this belief, and she now appreciates even her most difficult relationships as gateways for a greater understanding of herself as a spark of the divine living a human life.

One of the core principles that we share, and would like to invite you to consider, is that each one of us is born wanted. As we said in the opening of the book, the fact that we *appear* means that we are wanted, desired, worthy, and loved. A spot has been claimed for us by divine creation itself. To remove the obstacles that obscure this truth can take years, even lifetimes. Loyal to beliefs like "growth is difficult" and "love is painful," many of us struggle far too long within our relationships. It's as if we believe we're earning invisible merit badges for our agony.

In that sense, we would like to help speed the process of remembering your innate worthiness by taking you by the hand through this part of our journey together, to remember that while not all relationships are meant to last, every one of them that brings us closer to ourselves is worthwhile. Every one of them that brings us closer to God is worthwhile.

Understanding the core dynamics beneath our intimate relationship conflicts is one of the gateways that this book offers. These conflicts can surge up as arguments, co-dependent patterns, impasses, and the countless reasons for break-ups and divorces

Jack and Marion

Several years ago, Andy worked with a couple that has remained vivid in his memory. Jack was a partner in a top law firm in Washington, D.C., and his wife, Marion, was working on her Ph.D. in psychology at that time. Jack came from a family that was governed by a very old-fashioned father who would say things like, "Tears in men are not for the eyes of women." Jack's father saw it as one of his responsibilities to toughen up his son.

Marion was sexually abused by her father when she was growing up, which led to a distrust of men and difficulty communicating when old feelings of shame, unworthiness, and powerlessness were triggered. In fact, when they first began therapy, both Jack and Marion had great difficulty talking about their feelings and innermost needs and desires.

In his professional life, Jack felt like the odd man out. While his colleagues seemed to be concerned only about money, that didn't bring him the fulfillment and satisfaction that it was supposed to. He tried to fit into the hard-driving mold but it didn't work for him. For a long time, Jack fought the internal battle, trying to conform at the expense of his authentic self.

One of Marion's complaints was that Jack was distant and unavailable. They had three children, and for a long time she was upset that he would spend more time with their son, playing ball, than with their two daughters. She didn't yet understand how his upbringing instilled in him a belief that this is what fathers do.

Marion's upbringing was so full of disappointments and traumas, it became commonplace for her to complain, and Jack soon learned to expect it. Sometimes he even misinterpreted her communication as complaining when she wasn't. For example, sometimes when they would make love, she would say, "We should do this more often." Whereas she meant this as an expression of her enjoyment and appreciation for sharing this closeness with him, he took it as a criticism. He heard her saying that she didn't get enough time, attention, or sex rather than what she really meant: that it was wonderful and she wanted more of a good thing! At the most essential level, Marion wanted to be cherished and cared for (and was more interested in the quality of time together than the quantity), and Jack wanted to be understood and seen for who he really was.

The big change in their relationship came when Jack recognized that he really did have feelings and that he needed to take responsibility for them. One day he cried in Andy's office for the first time in decades. Marion began to see Jack differently. She learned things about his story that she hadn't known, and began to have more compassion for him. He too learned more about how she had grown up, including the fact that she had survived multiple sexual assaults at the hands of the man she was supposed to be able to trust with her life—her father. It actually took nearly 20 years for Marion to share this with Jack.

As his compassion for her deepened, she blossomed. As he opened up more and shared his authentic self, she melted. He too began to thrive in their renewed relationship where he felt respected and seen in a new light.

Jack ended up leaving the firm to go out on his own, and Marion started a consulting company. Not long ago, Andy ran into them after several years had passed. They said they had embraced the paradox that they are both "perfectly imperfect" and are doing great now. When they first came to Andy, they were on the brink of divorce. Now, after more than 25 years of marriage, they know that although they can offer infinite gifts of love to one another, happiness is in their own hands individually; it comes from the inside out, not the outside in.

Unfinished Business

Who we are today is a breathtaking and mysterious compilation of all the experiences we have had, along with the past lives that are a part of our soul's path home. These experiences combine to influence how we come to the door of our relationships, and what we do when we get inside. If we want to better understand our reactions to current situations, we can take a look at how we have already lived.

If our parents argued frequently and were unable to find agreeable resolutions, we might find ourselves avoiding conflict. This dynamic might echo a similar scenario from other lifetimes. Perhaps we have several life experiences where differences were met with disrespect and hostility. When we have felt trapped in a negative cycle with a partner in this life, maybe we were reacting to a previous life when we felt persecuted in a relationship and couldn't find a way to free ourselves from the torment. In Buddhist terms, it might be our karma to work through these conflicts in order to complete a pattern that we've carried within our souls.

Without recognizing our relationship challenges as opportunities to advance our souls, it's understandable that we would be fearful of conflict and avoid it as much as possible. This avoidance can appear in many forms. Some people drink to ease the anxiety of potential conflict. Others find solace in the arms of another person. It's not our partner we are running away from, but rather the unease we feel inside, which surfaces when we are reminded of past discomfort or pain. We would like to blame our partner for creating our bad feelings, but the truth is that we keep recreating these feelings ourselves by not turning toward our unresolved emotions with love. We wish our partner would not push those "hot" buttons in us, but without an understanding of how and why they get pushed, it's hard to prevent it.

Like most of us, Marion and Jack in the previous story were both struggling with unfinished business from their formative years. In psychological terms, this is an example of the *transference* that happens when our "unfinished business" is transferred from one relationship to another. There were unattended and unresolved emotional wounds derived from the past that had taken up residence in the present. Naturally, what we yearned for as children and couldn't have, we often yearn for as adults. We go about trying to obtain those things from a matrix of thinking where the wires have been seriously crossed. Expectations are turned upside down. We *expect* to encounter blockages and resistance. And we *don't expect* to get what we most deeply want. We expect to get hurt. And we don't expect to have the time of our lives.

Brian, a client of Andy's, is another example of how unfinished business wreaks havoc on intimate relationships. Brian was raised by a father who was very hard to please. Whenever Brian would express himself in a manner that was different than what his father desired, Brian was met with open scorn. Brian happened to be a superb tennis player, which his father felt was a waste of time. He would often silently toss his racquet out his bedroom window and sneak out to play when his father wasn't looking. Throughout Brian's life, he never felt he could please his father. As he grew older and started to date, he was drawn to women who were also hard to please. If he met a woman who was easy to please, he quickly became bored and lost interest. Although he is now in his sixties and has never married, his relationships with women are healthier and more enriching than at any other point in his life. As his awareness of the dynamic with his father has deepened, all of his relationships have benefited; and the cycle of approval, criticism, and rejection no longer feels like home.

Feeling Neglected

When we have had a history where our emotional needs were carelessly disregarded or met with blank indifference, we can become easily angered when we perceive that our partner isn't paying enough attention to us: "It's no different than when I was growing up! Sometimes he doesn't even know I'm in the same room."

Feeling neglected by our partner can bring old feelings quickly to the surface, sometimes taking us by surprise as we "over-react" to a relatively minor situation. We might say things to our partner that we secretly wish we could have said to our father or mother. Like Jack, whose father had also been raised by a critical and stoic man, it can hasten the healing process to realize that our parents were products of their environments as well. If, for a moment, we could see our parents and our partners as little boys and girls and consider how they were treated, we could be relieved of the pressure of taking everything they do or say so personally. Looking with empathy, resentment and even hate can transform to compassionate understanding.

Rebelling

If our partner makes a demand on us and we find ourselves rebelling against them like an adolescent, we might be unaware at that moment that their tone of voice reminds us of a harshness we heard in our mother's voice when she was aggravated with our father. Or it could be the other way around, where our father's voice was hard and full of judgment when he was angry with our mother. In either case, we wished so desperately in those early years that one of them would have stood up for themselves and not been a victim; and that the other parent would have been willing to step beyond their own self-centered world long enough to see the damage they were doing, and then stop it.

We may still be struggling with the tyranny we witnessed as a child, always fighting or defending ourselves against the "enemy." Or we may

111

be rebelling by exiting the situation; by drinking, over-working, leaving, or acting in any number of ways in order to stop our inner pain. Although we may be facing a situation with our partner right now that involves real problems, our *reaction* to the current situation is likely being directed by what the situation *reminds us of*. Our immediate desire is to stop what we believe to be the source of our pain, which has to be our partner, right? All logical indicators point in their direction! However, the real source is often emanating from our past. And since our emotions often don't know the passing of time, we re-live the pain from our memory of past events.

By recognizing where these trigger points come from, we can stop our knee jerk reactions and begin to respond more skillfully and appropriately to the current situation and create a true and lasting healing. When we hear that tone of voice, see that look in someone's eye, or feel that icy-cold shoulder across the room, we can make a new choice to respond in a way that we wished our parents would have back then. We may have been powerless then, but now we have the power of choice.

Unrealistic Expectations
How many awkward or horribly tense moments have involved making demands on our partners to fulfill desires and needs that were not theirs to fulfill? Without honestly facing our earlier experiences so that we can integrate them into a new adult perception, we can tend to make fairly outrageous demands on our partners. As most of us are basically good and loving people, we aren't consciously trying to cause trouble. But we can get into hot water because of our unrealistic expectations of what a relationship can or should do for us.

As a simple awareness practice, take a moment to contemplate how some of the following expectations have appeared in your significant love relationships (whether you were the one making the silent demand or the one on the receiving end):

Give me the happiness I never had.
Make up for the pain I experienced as a child.
Make me feel safe.
Read my mind.
Watch for and anticipate my needs.
Be aware of and sensitive to my feelings all of the time.
Put me first all of the time.
Don't ever betray me.
Don't ever hurt me.
Don't ever leave me.

The truth is that our partner doesn't make us feel the things we feel; we create feelings from within ourselves. No one can press our emotional buttons without our permission. Of course, that doesn't mean that they don't have a responsibility to treat us with dignity and care, but that is another matter. Empowerment comes from owning that we do have control where our feelings are concerned.

Cyndi and Andy both encounter clients who blame their partners for the way they feel. Although events can occur and things can be said that understandably stir up uncomfortable emotions, it is the way we *filter* those situations, behaviors, and words that cause us to feel and react in the ways that we do. We may find it hard to control our feelings because of previous programming, but blaming our partner only keeps us on a rollercoaster ride that we're probably tired of riding. Getting off the ride and becoming emotionally empowered brings us again to that all-important choice point. It requires a recognition that we may not always be able to control our feelings, but we do have control over our reactions—and we can *choose* how we are going to react.

When we contemplate our feelings (which often requires having a little space and time, like taking a walk or a hot bath), we can decide how to proceed thoughtfully rather than reflexively. And if we still feel mentally imprisoned by our own position of blame and righteousness, we can look for inspiration from others who have broken free. The profound Austrian analyst Viktor Frankl once said, "The last of human freedoms is to choose one's attitude in any given set of circumstances."

The Energetics of Co-Dependence

Unrealistic expectations and demands are built upon a ground of unresolved emotions. When we're in the midst of a difficult relationship—or a difficult passage within a relatively harmonious relationship—we often find a great deal of emotional confusion. In the middle of a storm, it may seem almost impossible to stop the "insanity" long enough to untangle and clarify how we're feeling and why. Sometimes it's too confronting or frightening. For example, while it may be easy to state that we're angry, identifying and expressing the feelings that exist beneath the anger may be far more daunting.

Anger can take many different forms, such as irritation, resentment, bitterness, cynicism, guilt, and sometimes resignation. As unique emotions along the spectrum of anger, each has its own story to tell. But go a little deeper and we will usually find the deeper emotions that anger is trying to protect us from feeling. Beneath anger's many guises, we may find anxiety, fear, sadness, loneliness, hurt, disappointment, remorse, or other more challenging feelings.

When we're able to look for a moment with objectivity, we can see that anger is always calling for some kind of change. It is asking for a behavior change, a belief change, an attitude change, or a change in perception within *ourselves*. And it's always calling us to a deeper level of honesty with ourselves and with the people we love. As compelling as it is to focus on what the other person *should* change, that really isn't under our control. What we can control and change are our own thoughts, feelings, beliefs, choices, and actions.

In Cyndi's counseling practice, she regularly observes the tendency in women to absorb the feelings and energies of everyone around them. This energetic tendency leads to psychological tendencies—and this is co-dependence in the making. Certainly, men can fall into this pattern too, but more often it is women who literally absorb what others aren't feeling, expressing, or owning. The male tendency is to play the role of *counter co-dependent*, where a man will often display an emotional stiffness and an unwillingness to acknowledge that he has any needs. This is one of the hardest dances to break in relationships. Women "absorbing" and men "not owning" is a centerpiece of the basic drama beneath relationships. In the quest for togetherness, it's a dance that eventually needs to stop. No one thrives in a codependent relationship; they only deepen the negativity, resentments, and addictions of the two people involved.

How does one create relationships that connect and bond instead of strangle and humiliate? We believe that as women can say, "This *isn't* mine," and men can say, "This *is* mine," then we will know that we are making great progress. In chapter 4, we explored the energetic boundaries that serve as mechanisms for protection but are also the means by which we share our deepest selves. These boundaries are essential as we determine what we will allow ourselves to absorb or not, and what we will claim ownership of or not. And in the quest to create healthy boundaries, it's inspiring to remember that the point is to increase our capacity to love and be loved—not to defend ourselves against it.

With all the strides we have made toward understanding the contrasts between men and women—especially over the past 50 years of social change, psychological breakthroughs, and spiritual growth—we still fall into the power-struggle pit together. This is true for gay and lesbian couples too, with one person usually expressing the masculine polarity and the other person expressing the feminine. By understanding the basic differences between the masculine and feminine polarities, we may be strengthened to pull ourselves out of the swamp of co-dependence when we find ourselves there, and better prepared to walk together in the wide-open field of interdependence.

Polar Shift

The unfinished business that gets transferred from family of origin onto our current relationships, from our past onto our present and our future, could most simply be described as one long wrestling match. Although some of us might have bright smiles, well-modulated voices, and bookshelves full of enlightenment teachings, let's face it: in certain ways, we are fighters. We fight to right the wrongs of the past. We fight to be heard, seen, and understood. And we fight the differences between us rather than appreciating them, enjoying them, and making the most of them. Some of us fight at high volume, shouting and yelling, while some of us get deadly quiet, passive-aggressively punishing our partners. Where we are headed now, at this half-way point in the book, involves an important shift in how and why we fight: Instead of fighting *against*, it's time now to fight *for*. Instead of fighting against our pasts, our parents, our ex-lovers, our current partners, and even against ourselves, now we can fight for awareness, understanding, clarity, and the freedom these can bring to our hearts.

At the start of this chapter, we referenced the duality that we're immersed in every day as we perceive life through an ego that is wired to see itself as separate from everything else. We live in the world as separate individuals where our partners, loved ones, and everyone else are separate from us. And as much as we see the world around us, we also sense the world within us.

One of the most extraordinary expressions of this duality is found in the dance between the masculine and feminine principles. With women typically embodying the feminine principle and men typically embodying the masculine principle, understanding these aspects as polar ends of one magnificent life force is a key to the clarity we seek.

This is the clarity that lights the way to loving—where we are free to end the battle with our opposites.

Influenced by Greek mythology, Jungian psychology elegantly depicts the goddess Eros as the feminine principle and the god Logos as the masculine principle. While Eros is the keeper of the gifts of relatedness and feeling, Logos holds the power to analyze, discern, and judge. As we know from experience, feelings and subjectivity are generally the domain of women, and logic and objectivity are generally the domain of men. Given that every man and woman possesses both the masculine and feminine principles as a part of their divine design, it's as if we're in a continuous dance with these two poles of expression, externally and internally. Jung described this with beautiful simplicity, saying that "life is founded on the harmonious interplay of masculine and feminine forces, within the individual human as well as without." The poignant search for the "self" that each of us embark upon involves these two opposite forces finding a dynamic balance within us.

Think about the way that natural forces in the physical world flow between two poles. Just as the North and South Poles of the earth create a force of magnetism, the masculine and feminine poles between people create a force of magnetism as well. While sexual energy is one important aspect of this magnetism, even it is one expression of a creative force that knows no bounds. In its most pure form, the feminine force is infinite energy moving freely, unobstructed in its magnificent ability to create, destroy, and recreate all that is. Where the feminine can be found shining its radiant light in many directions, the masculine moves in one direction—toward an expanse of consciousness that encompasses all that is. This is the infinite dance of yin and yang. And much more than a cool symbol adopted by the hippy counterculture, the simple image of two separate halves enfolding into one another—always separate and always one—is an outer representation of a dynamic that influences our lives on a daily basis.

We are literally and figuratively looking for our other half. We say things like, "He makes me feel whole," or "She completes me." Most often, we're attracted to the part of us that seems to be missing. We're attracted to qualities and traits that will make us whole. There is a Hebrew term, "tikkun olam," which is used today to refer to social action and the pursuit of justice; bringing society and ourselves back together into a harmonious and unified force for good. It refers to a "repairing" of that which has been divided. This is also a lovely description of what is happening within each one of us; a repairing of the wound of separation and a gathering of light, soul, and spirit. Remembering this could help us to approach our partners with greater honor, respect, and kindness.

The Power of Acceptance

As the authors of this book, if we could step through the pages and slip into chairs next to you, we are certain that we would have a fascinating conversation with you about your relationship journey. Although there are storylines that sound similar, every one of us experiences life in a unique and intensely personal way. We say this as a way to invite you into a more compassionate conversation with yourself about the pain you have experienced in loving others. In case you may be so inclined, we ask that you not relegate your own difficult relationships and relationship patterns to some forgotten corner of your mind or use them against yourself to punish yourself. Instead, we ask that you consider what bright possibilities could make themselves visible to you if you bring the sweetness of acceptance to everything you have gone through.

One of Cyndi's clients, Justine, recalled the time when her first love broke up with her when she was 17 years old. Although they had shared a vulnerable tenderness together as young lovers, Justine thoroughly expected him to break up with her. Deeply steeped in shame, she couldn't believe that this boy fell in love with her for one day, let alone several months. When it ended, the lights went out in her heart for a long while. It took over a year before she felt she had her head above the grief-filled waters she had been swimming in. As an adult, Justine has chosen men very much like the boy she fell in love with in high school. They have tended to be worldly, adventurous, bright, interested in spiritual development, and unavailable to be in a long-term relationship with Justine. She has a string of ex-boyfriends whom she considers friends now, but hasn't found her life partner.

Justine has looked at her relationship dynamics from, quite possibly, every angle imaginable. She has dissected her family of origin, had past life readings, focused on healing the shame and rage of the sexual abuse that she experienced as a young girl, and taken responsibility for how her patterns have become her safe zone. At this point, Justine is working with Cyndi to rest in a depth of acceptance that she had not known before now. More than simply admitting what has been played out in her most difficult relationships, Justine is embracing the lessons they have provided and forgiving herself and her previous partners for the pain that was perpetuated. The shift for her is one of choosing to turn toward gratitude as her point of reference for her relationships. While she is honest with herself about the patterns, she is letting go of her story about who she is in relationship to men. Justine has looked at the drama beneath her pasts loves and is now charting a new course.

Some of the questions that Justine has worked with to cultivate acceptance might be pertinent for you as well. As you read them, we invite you to see which ones resonate most strongly and use them for your own integration and healing:

In my relationship with_____, what is the most important lesson I have learned?

In thinking about the purpose of that relationship, what is the most empowering interpretation I can choose?

What was the greatest gift I received from being with him/her? What am I most grateful for about that relationship?

I forgive_____for_____.

I forgive myself for_____.

The Grace of Gratitude

Are you currently in a state of exhaustion and weariness from the relationship difficulties you have lived? We want to leave you with a candle of hope that you can carry with you into the chapters ahead. If you feel caught in a riptide of cynicism and resignation and cannot see a way out of the patterns you've come to identify with so closely, know this: You can be free.

There is a force that has the power to pick you up off the floor and set you down again in the center of your life. It is *gratitude*. To receive the benefits of this powerful medicine you have only to own the lessons and accept the gifts of wisdom that your challenging relationships have brought to you.

It is gratitude that puts you in direct connection with the Spirit that has been tending to your life since the moment you fell just a little ways from the Oak Tree.

So, with that in mind, what are you grateful for? And who are you grateful for? Holding the awareness of these in your heart can alter the fabric of your life.

Andy has made it an essential practice each night to take stock of what he's grateful for. Like a prayer, focusing on what he's grateful for puts him in what he describes as a state of grace. No fancy ritual involved. Just a deep inner "thank you." Cyndi's gratitude practice is in the *doing*. She likes to demonstrate her gratitude through action. A phone call, a card, an email, a hug—she likes to show her gratitude whenever possible. Explore what feels right to you, and see how gratitude can restore your faith, hope, and trust in relationships…and in yourself.

A Reflective Moment

In the 12-Step tradition of addiction recovery, there is a beloved prayer cherished by millions of people around the world that is known simply as the Third Step Prayer. Transcending religious dogma, it is a soulful request of the Divine that has the uncanny ability to lift us out of the limited perception of the ego and lead us into a wide, open field of faith, gratitude, and generosity of heart.

God, I offer myself to Thee —
to build with me and to do with me as Thou wilt.
Relieve me of the bondage of self, that I may better do Thy will.
Take away my difficulties, that victory over them
may bear witness to those I would help of Thy Power,
Thy Love, and Thy Way of life.
May I do Thy will always.

CHAPTER 7
ATTRACTING THE DREAM

Our truest life is when we are in dreams awake.
–HENRY DAVID THOREAU

What is it that brought you to this book, this conversation, this inquiry into intimate love? Is it a dream of deep fulfillment with the love of your life? Is it the desire for a relationship that inspires you to reach for the heights of your potential? Or is it a vision you hold for a quality of intimacy that adds pleasure and joy to your days? Whatever it is that got you to these pages, *it matters.* The whole point here is to support you in manifesting, attracting, and reveling in your heart's deepest desires.

Whether you are in a companion relationship or not, there are spiritual perspectives and practical action steps for attracting the "dream relationship" that we are eager to share with you. With your willingness to make the necessary changes inside and outside to be ready for your "true soul mate," you can relax and know that he or she could very well be on their way. If you are currently in a relationship, the new behaviors and attitudes that we're about to reveal *will* alter that relationship, inviting positive change at every level.

Where Dreams Meet Vision
We often hear the terms "dreams" and "vision" used interchangeably,

but we know intuitively that there is a difference. Yet they are akin to one another; we know that as well. It's as if they are our personal Holy Grails, calling us forward throughout our lives. Although the function and meaning of dreams and vision is intricate, we offer you a compact description to take with you as you move into the pages ahead.

Dreams are of the soul. They are the amalgamation of feelings and qualities of being that express the unique signature of our souls. Dreams help us to *feel* beyond what we have experienced before.

Vision is of the spirit. Like a view from the mountaintop, vision is a rendering of our dreams in the form of specific images, often illuminating the choices and actions that will help us to manifest our dreams in the outer world. Vision lights our way, allowing us to *see* beyond what we have experienced before.

Neither dreams nor visions are meant to be end results—of a relationship, a creative project, a career, a friendship, or even a life. It's not about obtaining them and then checking off the boxes: Dream. Check. Vision. Check. Instead, they are meant to add color, texture, beauty, and light to every step we take; along each of the paths that we've decided are important to us. For some, dreams and visions focus around work, career, and community. For others, dreams and visions constellate around raising a family and creative self-expression. And, of course, there are countless variations on the theme.

When it comes to romantic love, what is the dream you've carried with you throughout your life? What have you most wanted to experience and share with another person? Would you say that you're living your dream now, or do you feel like it's ever so close, like you can feel its imminent arrival? Or, do you feel like you've lost touch with your dream of togetherness, like a hazy memory from the distant past?

In a very real way, one of the primary purposes of this book is to evoke, clarify, and welcome your relationship dream. This is so vitally important. Your dream, as well as the vision that can support you in manifesting it, is a gift that your soul and spirit want you to receive. No doubt, you are well acquainted with the snowflake analogy that reminds us that there is only one YOU in the universe. Well, it stands to reason that your relationship dream is also one-of-a-kind. Only one person in all of existence can love your dream and fulfill it, and that is you.

So, let's get started! First we'll explore the desires and intentions that are integrally connected to your dream. And then we're going on a magic carpet ride, of sorts. We're going to take you on a tour of what we refer to as the garden of attraction—a place of aliveness, peace, and serenity. Although Botox, washboard abs, and making lists of specific attributes you want your partner to have can be lots of fun, nothing in the universe is as alluring as a heart that is open.

Desire & Intention

Our desires and intentions are intimately connected in the creation of our lives and loves. Unfortunately, desire has gotten a bad rap from various religions and spiritual traditions as being a human weakness that drags us around by the ear, making us want bad things and do bad things. But that is a terribly small view of a boundless creative force. Desire is a longing—a holy wanting—with a sacred source; like a fire in the heart that was lit by God. Desire has us turn our gaze toward the people, places, and experiences that bring fulfillment to the soul. It's when desire is denied that it stands the risk of becoming a twisted and toxic version of itself, morphing into cravings, compulsions, and addictions.

Intentions are the crystallized thoughts and the clear, positive statements of the outcomes we want to experience. They provide an internal framework for aligning with the activities and resources that will help us to manifest our goals. Intentions are paramount to bringing the non-physical into the physical. When we put an intention "out into the universe," we mysteriously find that there are energies out there to support it.

Looking at it from an energy standpoint, our dreams and desires are held by the feminine principle within each of us (whether woman or man), drawing to us that which is in alignment. While our vision and our intentions are held by the masculine principle that is within each of us, catalyzing our choices and actions. In short, dreams and desires attract, while vision and intentions direct.

Elements of Surprise

Cyndi was teaching a class once where she had the participants keep miracle journals. Among other things, they were using the journals to express their desires and clarify their intentions in key areas of their lives. One woman wrote down that she wanted a red Corvette. A few weeks later, she informed the group that she had indeed received her little hot rod. She described to everyone how she had gone for a walk on the beach. As she was enjoying the feel of the sand between her toes, she stepped on something sharp that caused her foot to bleed. When she put her hand in the sand to find the object she had stepped on, she found a small M atchbox car...a little red Corvette!

One way to interpret this story is to assume that the message is about getting clearer; to say definitively, "I want a *real* red Corvette that I can actually drive." However, another message pertains to being open to how the universe might want to play, sometimes surprising us in delightful ways. For example, one of Cyndi's previous boyfriends had always been attracted to brunettes, and then...well, Cyndi came along with her ultra-blond hair. In addition to the inner qualities that he valued about her, he came to appreciate the fact that he could easily spot her in a dark movie theater. Her crown of hair was like a light bulb illuminating the path to his seat.

When Andy first got engaged to his wife, his mom protested, "A Lutheran farm girl from Iowa!? You could do better! You should be marrying a Jewish girl." His young fiancée didn't fit the picture that his mother had long held for him. However, both stayed open to new possibilities and the love and affection that grew between Tess and Andy's mom over the years was not to be held back by a few outdated pictures about how things were supposed to be. How things really *are*, when we don't fight against them, is always more enlivening than the way they *should* be.

Like a beautiful ballroom dance, we can enjoy our lives so much more if we're willing to allow our dreams, desires, visions, and intentions to dance too. Can we allow them to have the space to move, twirl, and take exciting turns on the dance floor? Can we allow them to change? Sometimes our dreams get woven together with others. Sometimes they don't come to fruition at all. We can't predict the timing—which year, decade, or lifetime something might come to pass. But it's important that we acknowledge how much of our dream *is* being realized and in what ways. The universe tends to support our deepest desires, but, as we've seen, not always in the way we envision them.

Our dreams and visions are living and breathing aspects of our deepest selves, not static pictures gathering dust in our minds. This is true whether one is 25 or 85. It's true whether single or partnered. We hold them in our bodies and our energy fields, as well as our hearts. And we express them through our thoughts, words, and actions. The particulars shift and change, but usually there are clear threads that run throughout our lives, weaving their way through time and space.

Since he was a young man, Andy has held an intention to have, as he puts it, *a simple love affair for sixty years*. And that is exactly what he's been sharing with his wife for forty years now.

The Garden of Attraction

Welcome to the garden. We're going to walk together through the lush and soul-sumptuous grounds of attraction. As you may have assumed, we're talking about a quality of attraction that includes far more than sexual attraction alone. To be clear, we're not downgrading sexual attraction to a more "lowly" measure on an invisible scale of importance. But the delight and thrill of sexual energy is perhaps only a taste of an aliveness that has the power to wake us out of the trances we sometimes find ourselves in. We slip into trances of stress, overwork, overwhelm, anxiety, competition, and other fear-based states of mind. What better to draw us out of a trance than something alluring and enlivening—a sound, a smell, a song, a person, or a moment that holds the promise of pleasure?

As our focus is on cultivating intimate relationships that bring us closer to ourselves, to others, and to life itself, we're approaching attraction from a deeper level of consciousness. We're exploring perspectives, attitudes, behaviors, and states of being that have the power to draw to you a love that fulfills and transforms you.

What attracts the quality of love and depth of experience that we're seeking? What is it that is vitalizing to the senses, enticing to the heart, seductive to the soul, and fascinating to the spirit?

The Heart That Overflows

On a physical level, we know that the heart requires blood and oxygen in order to function. But what does the heart need on an emotional and spiritual level? What does the heart really desire? On the deepest level, the heart wants to feel alive. When we feel joy, our awareness of the world is expanded. We notice more, feel greater generosity, and feel God's presence with greater intensity. This feeling occurs most when our heart connects with another heart.

Working with clients nearly every day who are either looking for their partner or wanting the one they have to make some changes, we waste no time getting to their core desires. Once we address the more superficial list of traits they want their partners to have (i.e., great job, healthy bank balance, tall, short, slim, muscular, well-traveled, etc.), the central desire could almost always be summarized this way: "I'm looking for someone who really enjoys life; someone in whose presence I feel more alive too."

Is there anything more attractive than someone who is radiantly and joyously alive?

Cyndi's closest girlfriends have noticed over the years how easily and effortlessly men are attracted to her. What's her secret? Although Cyndi's boundaries are crystal clear, she doesn't hide her profound appreciation for being alive. She doesn't stop her heart from overflowing, one to another. When it comes to the living of life, Cyndi's attitude is, "Let's feel it! Let's *grow* through it!"

It's important to be conscious of the conditioning that has lured us into believing that aliveness is something that can be "bought." Yes, we can certainly feel sparks of aliveness when we win the game, achieve the goal, receive the accolades, open the gift box, or make the big purchase. Those are exciting yet often fleeting moments. But if we look more closely, it's never really the "thing" itself that brings the aliveness. It's really how that thing connects us with others. We stop short, focusing on the commodity instead of the connection. The real source of the good feelings is overlooked and, suddenly, "the thrill is gone."

Countless times in their careers, Cyndi and Andy have heard clients explain why they are "done" with their relationships: "I warned him for years and years. And now the relationship is just dead." Her partner wakes up and tries to save it, but it's too late. The aliveness faded away; usually a gradual process with a good amount of emotional "numbing out." What they have both observed is that if there is anger, there is usually something to work with. Anger can be viewed as change trying to happen. If there's apathy, it's usually done. In the realm of intimacy and togetherness, apathy is the opposite of love.

To attract a new love into your life, or to attract a new depth of connection and togetherness in your existing relationship, let your heart take flight! Let it put on its dancing shoes! Look for things to be excited about. Anticipate good things happening. Have "taking care of yourself" include making plans and looking forward to things. Make enthusiasm and optimism consciousness priorities. And practice letting your heart overflow, especially in moments when you have good excuses not to.

Breaking All the Rules

Earlier, we stated that Cyndi's love of life is one of the secrets of her attractiveness, and now we'll break that down a little further.

Going back to her best girlfriends, they say that Cyndi gives off a light. But it's not just her bright hair and big smile they're referring to. The light comes from a willingness to be fully herself—the good, the bad, and the ugly. She knows herself very well, which, of course, includes being aware of her deficits. As she says, "I don't major in the minors." In other words, she doesn't put a lot of attention on her deficits. She says, "I let a lot of myself be as it is. Since I know myself pretty well and accept myself, I have nothing to hide."

This is a statement worth meditating upon: "Since…I accept myself, I have nothing to hide." Given the depth of shame, self-judgment, and self-loathing that most human beings are heir to, authentic self-acceptance is one of the most attractive qualities on earth. We are innately drawn to the possibility of knowing our wholeness.

One specific example of Cyndi's self-acceptance pertains to her sense of direction when driving…or lack thereof. She has no qualms admitting that she frequently gets lost when she's driving. She knows it, as does everyone who knows her well, and she puts no energy into covering up this truth. In fact, she says, "I go with it! My ex-husband has made it a habit to call me when I'm on my way somewhere with our son. He checks in to see how lost I am and has directions ready for me. Because I can chuckle about it, so can he."

Another example of Cyndi's self-acceptance is reflected in her relationship to her outer appearance. But first, a warning: This point may be highly controversial given our collective obsession with external perfection. However, we are willing to make a few waves for the sake of love and inner peace. Okay, so the brazen fact is that Cyndi doesn't really care what she wears.

There. We said it.

There is a woman in the civilized world who isn't thinking about what outfit she's wearing when she steps out her door. AND, she's a highly visible woman—teaching at a local college, leading workshops around the world, doing media interviews, and attending her sons sporting events multiple times each week. But the fact remains, Cyndi has been known to go out in public with her shirt inside out and her hair pulled back in a ponytail with rubber bands. Yet, in spite of sweatpants, messy hair, and no make-up, people engage with her. As Cyndi's comfort with herself is projected outward, people feel comfortable in her presence. Grocery clerks, kids, older people, and, yes, men too will happily talk with her. There is a wonderful naturalness about her.

One experience at a grocery store several years ago is an entertaining example of how having a sense of ease with oneself is highly appealing. Cyndi says, "I was with my oldest son and three of his friends; they were eight years old at the time. I'm sure it looked like I was the mother of quadruplets. I was wearing hiking boots, an old, long sundress, a huge straw hat, and no make-up. I looked a fright. I was breaking ALL the rules of how to meet a man, which was fine with me. All I wanted to do was buy food for lunch and get out of there with the same four boys I entered the store with. I think three men in total tried to engage in conversation with me before I walked out. It was silly."

When we aren't busy hiding who we are, people are drawn to the warmth and spaciousness that authenticity creates. Magical things happen. For one thing, when we're comfortable with our own quirks and eccentricities, we become more interesting to other people.

And it gets even better. When we're not tying up huge amounts of energy and focus attempting to get the rules of engagement right, we naturally find ourselves more *interested* in others. When a person is genuinely, whole-heartedly interested in others, their powers of attraction are unstoppable.

Peace and Serenity

When we are content with who we are, we hold a resonance of peace and serenity. Of course, when we talk about contentedness, we're not referring to complacency or resignation; not the "screw you if you don't like me" attitude that people will sometimes cite as an example of how they're now perfectly okay with themselves. No, we're referring to the Real McCoy, a tranquility of being that is palpable when we shift our attention away from our ego (which loves as much attention as it can get) and onto the gratitude that bubbles up effortlessly from the inner well of self-acceptance.

When we're kind to ourselves, we become less needy. We're more comfortable in our own skin. And our boundaries—although perhaps stronger than ever—get to evolve as well! Their focus shifts from boundaries that protect us from harm to boundaries that attract goodness beyond measure.

Within the brilliance of the 12-Step tradition, the entire goal is serenity no matter what is happening outside of a person. And one of the commitments is to hold oneself 100 percent responsible for progressing toward serenity—not perfecting the ability to be serene, but progressing toward it. This is a code for living that we would all do well to adopt.

Energetic Boundaries and the Beauty of Responsibility

Cultivating our powers of attraction does indeed come with a great deal of responsibility. As we consciously choose to be open, vulnerable, and receptive—paramount for having intimacy in our lives—we must simultaneously call on greater discernment in certain situations.

Tending to our energetic boundaries becomes a priority. Being increasingly clear about our perceptions and interpretations of situations and people becomes a priority. Approaching our decisions and choices mindfully becomes a priority. In the continuous dance between what is happening inside of us and what's happening outside of us, being attuned to the still, small voice within can no longer be ignored.

While the peace of self-acceptance can increasingly become our inner experience, there are certain triggers that will cause us to occasionally lose our serenity. This is when knowing ourselves well is essential. Self-honesty will dictate if we're able to be around people and situations that act as triggers or if they're likely to lead us down a path of self-abandonment.

For instance, Cyndi doesn't go to parties where alcohol is the main attraction. Although she occasionally has a glass of wine, she gets triggered when she is with people who are drunk. She takes full responsibility for how people being drunk can spark a disturbance for her on the inside. Knowing that it's not the job of a hostess or party-giver to decide if she can handle something or not, Cyndi decides whether to stay or go. She says, "If I'm not comfortable with the way someone is acting or being, I turn away. I stop a conversation. I move to the other side of a café. Or I leave that line if I'm in a store."

It's freeing to remember that we're not here to win a popularity contest. And it's empowering to remember that love has boundaries.

How to Meet Lots of Guys: *A Cautionary Tale*
If you're someone who is in the process of dating and wanting to meet new people, you'll probably appreciate the old sentiment that not every low-hanging piece of fruit should be picked. One of Cyndi's clients offers a memorable example of this folk wisdom.

When Rose was 15 years old, an angel appeared to her and told her that she would lose her first child. Fast-forward several years: Cyndi first met Rose right before she got married and had a child. She brought her daughter to see Cyndi when the little one was about one-year old, and Cyndi intuitively saw a dark spot in the child's brain. Rose brought her daughter to a doctor and she was diagnosed with a terminal brain tumor. She died six months later.

Rose was devastated and gained 20 pounds very quickly. It wasn't only the intense grief of losing her daughter that was weighing her down. She was also suffering the loss of her marriage. As it turned out, after her daughter was diagnosed, she discovered that her husband was having an affair. Soon after her daughter's death, she and her husband divorced.

After a while, when Rose began to have thoughts about finding love again, she admitted to Cyndi that she felt too drained and heavy to meet anyone. To reignite her vital life force, Cyndi first had Rose focus on "turning on" her first chakra, the potent root chakra of survival and sexuality. Working with visualization and meditation techniques to open this energy center, Rose met EIGHT men in TWO days.

Now, as fascinating as that was, as a teaching story, it gets even better. You see, it turned out that all of these men were more interested in sex than in close, intimate relationships. So, Cyndi and Rose knew that there was more work to do energetically. Using the color pink in her visualizations, Cyndi guided Rose to shift her focus to her fourth chakra, the heart center. Integrating the potency of her lower charkas with the grandeur of her heart, Rose's powers of attraction became aligned with her real dreams. A few months later, she was house-sitting for friends and met a fantastic man who lived next door with his two daughters. Today, Rose is married to him and helping to raise his girls.

Rose and her new man allowed their relationship to start slowly. Having endured some of life's most searing losses, they had both learned to deeply savor and appreciate their togetherness. They reveled in taking their courtship slowly and letting it evolve.

Andy and Cyndi have both observed in their work over the past three decades that relationships that start slower often last longer. Similarly, long-term relationships that are treated like a *continual courtship* are the best of all. (We will reveal "the continual courtship" in greater detail in chapter 12, so stay tuned.)

Honoring the Light in Others

The greatest "secret" for attracting the dream relationship comes down to a matter of light. Honoring the light in others is the most potent prescription we could offer. So what does it mean to honor the light in others? How does honoring manifest?

We honor the light in others by noticing it, by being interested in it, by acknowledging it, by caring about it, and by celebrating it. Most of all, we honor the light in others by allowing their light to change us for the better.

When we are genuinely interested in other people—and not only the men and women we might want to date, but people in general— we become more attractive. When we know that we are all equal, we become more attractive. When we value the people at our local coffee shop, at the bank, the grocery store, and the gas station equally, we become more attractive. How could we run our lives without them?! When we're truly accepting of others, and when we allow the growing ease within ourselves to create a place of ease for others, we become more attractive.

Most importantly, when we can embrace that everyone carries a divine light within, we become magnets for the highest expression of love.

Walking in the Light

So we have taken a brief walk together through the garden of attraction, and you may have noticed that there is a distinct quality to the air in this lovely "place." We could describe this metaphorical air as nourishing, fragrant, and light, like sitting by a waterfall in Hawaii surrounded by pikake flowers. Why is that? What is the primary "element" that makes such ease and self-acceptance possible? What is it about this atmosphere that helps our dreams, intentions, and desires to take flight? What is that sweetness that is wafting by? It's forgiveness.

When you forgive yourself for your mistakes and the ways that you may have harmed or abused yourself, you build an energetic bridge that enables you to walk out of your past and into the sunlight of the present. When you forgive the people in your life who have (knowingly or unknowingly) wounded your heart, you stop guarding it so fiercely. Freed from the weight of resentment and regret, you discover that you are more *present* with people than ever before—and presence is a very sexy thing.

A Reflective Moment

Take a moment to breathe, relax, and reflect. Think of an aspect of yourself that you have judged and criticized—a part of you that is longing for your self-acceptance. Allow yourself to imagine how you would feel if you were to embrace this part of you with warmth and kindness...if you were to love it. Then simply let yourself imagine how other people would respond to you from this place of greater self-acceptance.

CORNERSTONE III
Togetherness with a Current Partner

THE THIRD CORNERSTONE of togetherness is
focused on how to continuously nurture and artfully
sustain the relationship you already have. Part III will
provide you with the perspectives and practices that
support the Together Couple. This section comprises
your togetherness toolkit, which can serve you in very
practical yet soul ways on a daily basis. Including a
simple assessment tool in chapter 8, you will go on a
transformative journey into the world of honoring—how
to honor your partner through change and transition;
through conscious communication; and through a whole-
hearted acceptance of who they are. Discover forgiveness,
appreciation, and optimism as the recipe for a truly
successful partnership. The culmination of this section
is a poignant exploration of sex in the life of the together
couple, a rekindling of the emotional connection that
leads to lasting passion.

CHAPTER 8
THE TOGETHER COUPLE

*Wake at dawn with a winged heart and give
thanks for another day of loving.*
–KAHLIL GIBRAN

We have just come from an exploration of what it takes to attract the quality of togetherness that we truly want—our heart's deepest dream for connection and wholeness. Now we set about on the road to explore what sustains that dream. What nourishes and supports the deepening of love over time? What is the special alchemy that transmutes our desires into the relationship we have envisioned for ourselves?

Every successful relationship is composed of several practical and spiritual factors, which combine to formulate togetherness. For couples and individuals, this chapter describes these basic qualities and illuminates their meaning and purpose in developing relationships that enrich your life.

This informative chapter will give you ideas and perspectives that you can put to use right away, as well as contemplate over time. If you are in a partnership right now, the relationship necessities described here will help you to observe and assess its current condition. Ultimately, they will lead you to deepening the bonds that honor, nurture, and sustain great love. And if you aren't currently in a romantic partnership, you can study, practice, and hone the described qualities in your other relationships. After all, love is love.

A Question of Perspective: *Enhancing Rather than Fulfilling*
Why is it so hard to sustain a satisfying relationship? One reason is because we ask our partners (often without saying a word) to fulfill us in ways that they aren't meant to. You'll understand what we mean when you review the following wish list, which the vast majority of us can relate to:

We want to be loved in a way that fills our heart and soul.
We want to be loved in a way that heals the pain of the past while
   fulfilling our desires to feel complete.
We want to feel understood, valued, and attended to on multiple
   levels—physically, emotionally, and spiritually.
We would like to do the same for our partner.

On paper, it seems easy enough. So why doesn't it work much of the time? Because we have needs and desires that other people can't fulfill, and others have needs and desires that we can't fulfill. For too many years we go in search of a mother or father substitute—to either pick up where ours left off or to give us the perfect love we sought from them but never received. Our partner can't be our mother, our father, or our bank.

As obvious as this statement is, it's important to shine a clear light on it because of the tremendous amount of conditioning we've received to the contrary since the day we were born. We can't heal another person; we can only support their healing.

Healing occurs from the inside out, not the reverse. Certainly, outer circumstances can support and hasten healing, but the process happens within our own thoughts, feelings, perceptions, and energy fields. Similarly, satisfaction comes from the inside out too. The cup that is to be filled to overflowing is within the sanctum of our own hearts. As we tend to our own lives with greater care and self-respect, negative states of consciousness begin to slide away. As emotional states such as worry, jealousy, self-pity, and resentment soften and dissipate, a space opens up within us to receive love and the attention that accompanies it.

Our partner's love is the icing on the proverbial cake, not the cake itself. So it is true, we do have to love ourselves first. This is precisely why we dedicated the first several chapters of this book to exploring and nourishing the relationship we each have with ourselves. In most cases, our mothers attempted to fulfill our needs in the beginning of our lives. Now it is up to us. To attract and sustain the depth of intimacy that will help us to heal and evolve, we have to walk in the shoes of our adult selves.

Giving love is about discovering and knowing what enhances our partner's life, not trying to fulfill them completely. Likewise, letting ourselves be loved is about understanding what enhances our own lives and being willing to allow our partner to contribute to that—*not asking them to fulfill us.*

Also, knowing where, when, and how to be a supportive partner takes time and patience. *Through talking, listening, and observing, we can come to understand the very being of the man or woman who is our mate.*

When we let ourselves move more fluidly between our longing to live a life of profound meaning and the desire to simply have fun, we realize the truth—that we are each multi-faceted human beings. We are both simple and complex, and our needs and desires reflect this.

As we cultivate an understanding that our partner can enhance our life but is not responsible for fulfilling it, it's as if we open a window and what breezes in but a refreshing clarity. This awareness can forever alter the quality of our relationship. It can also reorient us to the real power of responsibility and choice in our lives. Rather than being seen as heavy obligations that drag us down, responsibility and choice can now be perceived as some of the sweetest solutions we will ever know. As we extend love to ourselves, we become increasingly receptive to the love of the other. Like a thirsty plant that has been watered, our petals open up to receive the bounty of love that life is offering us night and day.

How different is that perspective from the one where we view responsibility as a weight that we're fated to drag around if we dare to be in love? We *can* choose to leave behind this "sad sack" story and go for a more loving and lively fairy tale. We don't have to settle for the plot line that says committed relationships eventually become a ball and chain of aggravation, boredom, and disappointment.

As we are about to find out, *that* perspective is a choice too, as are all perspectives.

The Togetherness Commitment:
Welcoming Responsibility and Embracing Choice
Imagine the beauty of making a commitment to your beloved that goes something like this...

> *My love, I promise to take responsibility for my own needs and desires—to come to know them and express them honestly. I promise to warmly welcome responsibility, knowing that this willingness will guide me toward my own fulfillment and allow me to care deeply about yours. With this commitment, I will turn my potential into loving power through the quality of my day-to-day choices. The more joyously I respond to my inner world, the greater my capacity to receive your love... and the greater my capacity to love you.*

As you can see, we're referring to a responsibility that uplifts and enlivens, not the false responsibility that can be used as a way to punish ourselves, which is captured by the phrase, "I made my bed, now I've got to lie in it." One of the primary purposes of exploring the wounds of childhood, including the many faces of shame and fear that we carry into adulthood, is to free ourselves from this type of heavy-duty responsibility.

With our respective counseling clients, we observe great success in relationships when both partners are willing to take responsibility for their own happiness, and not begrudgingly but *willingly*. Responding to their own childhood wounds and the unmet emotional needs connected to them—and being aware of how their relationship is affected when they ignore this part of themselves—they find it much easier to see their partner more clearly. It's as if they might say, "*Oh*, you are not my mother, my father, my first love, or my even my ex-husband! I see you for who you are."

This is one of the greatest gifts we can give to another human being: to see and accept them as they are.

This depth of awareness opens the door internally to making more conscious choices in our relationships. Each day, the together couple chooses anew: "How will I view my partner today? How will I treat my partner today? I choose to see the best in them and to believe in their greatness. Each day I make a conscious choice to love them."

Practically every minute of every day, we make decisions and choices. Decisions are the assessments we make and the conclusions we come to based on our own beliefs and values. From those internal decisions, we make our choices (putting those decisions into action). Many of our choices are simple ones, like which socks to put on or which pen to pull from the cup on our desk. Other choices have greater consequences, like whether to eat ice cream or fresh fruit. When making choices that appear to have no measurable consequences, we take very little time deciding. We go with our intuition. Decisions that have greater consequences often take more time, as we measure whether the immediate gratification is worth the long-term impact. When buying a car, do we submit to our desire, impulsively throwing caution to the wind? Do we buy the little sports car with the big price tag, or do we take our time and research a car for its utility and best resale value? Choices, choices, choices.

Being in a relationship is a song of multiple notes as well. Every day we decide how we are going to treat our partner. Every day we orchestrate our behaviors so that we're in harmony or dissonance. Are we going to say whatever is on our mind even if it hurts their feelings? Or, are we going to think it through and measure the consequences of our words and actions?

It's easy to feel righteous and lash out when we feel hurt by our partner. We want to "stand up" for ourselves, and defending ourselves with harsh words can seem perfectly reasonable in the heat of the moment. But there comes a time, either as a relationship evolves or ends, when we open our eyes and understand that everything we say and do toward our partner has impact and consequences.

The "3 Times" Rule – *a communication practice*

When we feel hurt and angry with our partner, when we feel as though we have been mistreated or betrayed in some way, it's important to allow ourselves to express our upset feelings with honesty and self-responsibility.

When we *don't* do this, we're left with dismal alternatives: suppressing our feelings, obsessing over the perceived wrongdoing, lashing out, staying stuck in the past, and/or caught in a tape-loop of reliving the pain.

In working with many clients over the years who were suffering with Post-Traumatic Stress Disorder (PTSD), Andy has observed a similar repetitive cycle taking place. When we don't have the proper outlets for our emotions—when we continuously relive an event that has been injurious to us in body, mind, or spirit—we unknowingly create neural pathways that keep the pain in place.

We also find this same difficult pattern when there has been an infidelity in a relationship, where the person who has been "cheated on" gets stuck in a loop of painful mental pictures and overwhelmingly negative emotions.

Although there are many effective therapies and healing practices for addressing this dynamic of suppression, obsession, and pain, we would like to offer you a simple yet highly effective practice for unblocking emotions and moving forward. This practice can be useful in moments of minor irritation, as well as major emotional upset.

Identify: Briefly describe the thoughts, feelings, and emotions that you're experiencing.

Own: Claim that it's your responsibility to tend to your emotions and affirm that you have the ability to do so.

Express: Set a clear boundary that you will allow yourself to whole-heartedly *complain* about the situation a total of three times. Whether you share your "complaints" with a counselor, your partner, a friend, your journal, or some other receptive and willing party, allow yourself to be honest and uncensored.

New alternatives: Now that you've allowed yourself to express your emotional upset, what are you free to think about? What is the new, positive internal dialogue that can replace the painful dialogue? What else can you tell yourself?

Look ahead: Now, with a commitment to moving forward, what are the lessons and gifts that have come from this situation? How can you use what you've learned in the future?

One of the most significant choices we make in the context of our relationship is how we want to view our partner. In the beginning of a relationship, we see the best in our partner. We are forgiving, kind, and emotionally generous toward them. Over time, our perceptions can change. If we don't make it a priority to be emotionally honest and present, an accumulation of disappointments, complaints, grudges, and betrayals can taint our perceptions. Anger and self-righteousness can be a seductive elixir.

We can choose to see our partner as selfish and uncaring, justifying treating them unkindly. Or we can choose to view him or her as an extraordinary person dealing with ordinary human issues, which will likely produce better reactions toward them.

Which view of them is the right one? Perhaps both are correct. But the pivotal juncture is *choosing* what comes next. For example, imagine you're having a disagreement with your partner. You have important choices to make: *How will I speak to my partner? Is the healthy choice to stay in the room or take a walk around the block?* We all have the capacity to be kind or cold. Again, even if we don't like what they are saying or doing, we can choose to see the best in them. We can look deeper, beyond a word or action, and see the heart we fell in love with.

The choices we make regarding how we view our partner will dictate the climate of the relationship. What will today's weather report bring? Will the relationship be chilly and distant with distrust, or warm and balmy with affection?

Although we don't have the power to control other people (including their thoughts, feelings, decisions, choices, and behaviors), we do have *influence*. We can choose to be a compelling force for good in the lives of others. With our partner, we can witness magic happen when we choose to look through God's glasses again, to see the soul and spirit that is animating this precious human life.

Toward those goals, the remainder of this chapter will provide you with further tools and perspectives necessary for creating a divinely-inspired relationship, whether that's with your longtime partner or the beloved that you have yet to meet.

If you are currently in a relationship, the next section ("The Togetherness Assessment") will help you to see where you are right now along the spectrum of closeness and distance with your partner. It will give you an opportunity to observe the way you're communicating and how you're handling change in your relationships.

Once you have made your assessments, we will offer you a new view of the most important ingredients we know of for nurturing successful relationships: forgiveness, appreciation, and optimism.

The Togetherness Assessment: *Am I Honoring My Partner?*

Honoring our partner is a powerful way to bypass any ideas we may have about trying to "get it right" in relationship, "do it perfectly," or "say the right thing." Perfectionism (or even the notion that if we can just figure out the rules of the game, we'll know how to win it) is usually employed by the ego to keep us tethered to a pattern that feels safe but actually guarantees failure. Honoring another person, as well as ourselves, has nothing to do with getting it right.

What does it mean to honor your partner? In our head and in our heart, we make room for their existence. When we honor someone, we are respectful of their thoughts, feelings, and beliefs, and we're honest about our own. We're willing to be open, to listen, to know, and to understand. When we honor someone, we actively support their right to heal, grow, and change. In a sense, we could say that honoring another person is one of the greatest acts of kindness and generosity possible. In effect, it says, "I acknowledge that you are a sacred human being—infinitely worthy, whole, and complete—and I will treat you as such, even when I'm frightened or angry."

So, it is through this doorway of honoring that we invite you to examine some of the key areas of your relationship with your partner. And if you're not in a partnered relationship at this time, you can still use this assessment tool to observe your closest companion relationships, as well as your relationship with yourself.

At the end of the four summaries on communication, change, acceptance, and transitions, you will have an opportunity to look and see where you are right now (on a scale from 1 to 10) along the spectrum of creating and sustaining relationships of closeness, intimacy, kindness, and inspiration.

Honoring through Conscious Communication

Andy had a client at one time whose motto for her marriage was, "You go along, to get along." Aside from even a hint of passion, this disempowered formula also left out the need to honor and take care of herself. Outwardly, she took pride in the fact that she had been married for ten years and had never had one argument…until the day she left the marriage. Beneath the surface of calm and quietude, her emotional levy was filling up and came to an abrupt breaking point.

Because you are human, you are already well acquainted with the variety of communication styles that any one of us possesses. We are capable of a wide spectrum within a very short amount of time: from calm, measured reasoning; to crying and screaming; to numb confusion; to vulnerability and openness—and many variations in between.

One thing we hear from many of our clients and friends is a real curiosity about how other couples communicate. *Are other people arguing as much as we are? Is the harmony and ease in our relationship shared by many or few? How do we know if our conflicts are "normal" or cause for alarm? What does healthy, strong, and loving communication look like?*

Andy learned when studying the research of renowned psychologist John Gottman, Ph.D. that positive vs. negative interactions in happy couples is 20 to 1, in conflicted couples is 5 to 1, and in soon-to-be-divorced couples is .8 to 1. This important data helps to demystifies the way couples interact with each other, quantifying the difference between happy couples and couples in conflict.

As tempting as it may be in the heat of the moment to lash out and defend your position, practice communicating with more thoughtful specificity. Instead of making an accusation, describe the behavior that triggered you and explain how you feel as a result of it. Instead of starting sentences with "you," start with "I feel…" You state the event or experience, and then let the person know how you feel in relationship to it. In that way, there's no blame. As we have said, anger is change trying to happen. So trust this and avoid making inflammatory "always" and "never" accusations that can leave your partner feeling punished and misunderstood.

Earlier, we described the invitation that Andy extends to couples when they begin counseling with him—a basis of communication that honors the unique perceptions of both people and frees them from the bondage of blame: *You are not me, and we're both right.*

From that healthy starting point, the next question is really an opportunity: *Since we both matter and we're both going to be heard in this situation, how are we going to make things work for both of us?* One measure of a good relationship is not how well we get along but how well we resolve our differences. Differences don't have to turn into arguments.

If you're accustomed to conflict, you might be wondering how this is possible. When we're solving a problem or a disagreement, we must keep talking until we find consensus. Issues should be viewed through a team perspective, where the question is: How are *we* going to make this work for both of us? This question acknowledges that the values of both partners need to hold equal weight. Once decisions have been reached, it's important to make explicit agreements with one another. When created consciously and lovingly, agreements serve many beautiful purposes. For one thing, they give us a basis from which we can have positive expectations for the future.

Although it can take time to resolve our differences (and some may not get resolved at all), conflict is always an invitation into deeper understanding. In fact, the ultimate goal of a difference of opinion is closeness. Use those moments to discover more about what is meaningful to your partner and to learn their unique "language of love."

Communication Assessment

On a scale from 1 – 10 (with 1 being very little and 10 being a lot), circle the number that best answers the following question:

To what extent are you practicing conscious communication in your primary relationship?

1 – 2 – 3 – 4 – 5 – 6 – 7 – 8 – 9 – 10

Contemplation for Growth:
No matter what number you chose for yourself in this moment, what can you do to progress upward on the scale?

Honoring Change
Have you noticed how inconsistent many of us are when it comes to how we relate to change within our relationships? We could even use the word *fickle* to describe that vacillating motion, as we swing back and forth between

"please don't change; I feel safer when I know what to expect from you" and "if you don't change, I don't know if I can stand another day with you." This is barely an exaggeration, right?

Andy has a client who cannot accept that his wife is not as ambitious as he would like her to be. He has tried everything he can think of to get her to change and she hasn't. If he could give up on his mission and accept her as she is, he could feel more at peace. There are some traits that people can change and some they just can't. It isn't always a matter of will. Sometimes it's just who we are. In the case of Andy's client, is it possible that his idea of what ambition looks like is obscuring his ability to see his wife's version of ambition? She seems content with their life together. But this is not good news to him. Some people believe that contentment breeds complacency, which is feared to be one step away from a life sentence of horrific boredom and monotony. The truth is that one can be content and still be ambitious. Also, what undiscovered enchantments might his wife possess that his eyes are closed to while he's preoccupied with how she needs to change? In any case, he's learning one of the central truths of relationship: You can't change another person, only yourself.

On the other hand (and this is one of the big, often unspoken fears in relationships), there is the quiet dread that if our partner does change, our relationship with them will suddenly be on shaky ground. Subconsciously, so much stock is put into the idea that predictability means safety, and anything that alters the map that we use to navigate our relationship can be perceived as a threat. Maybe you have experienced this firsthand? One of you gets a promotion at work; one of you loses weight and puts more energy into looking good; one of you receives a windfall of money, and all of the congratulations and words of praise (which may be quite sincere) are painfully tainted by the fear of rejection or loss. The *what if's* set in, like "What if she wants to trade me in for a newer model?"

Another poignant example of this type of fear is when one partner goes into treatment to address an addiction, usually an alcohol or drug addiction, and the non-using partner confronts an unsettling and secret thought that can sound like this: "When my husband is clean, sober, and strong again, he might see that he doesn't need me anymore. He might see my flaws and leave." These are examples of how we can give our power away to the unresolved wounds of yesterday and opt-in to a life of codependency.

As we discussed earlier, we're conditioned to cling to safety at all costs. But what we really want, in our deepest heart, is to feel alive. And change is a core aspect of aliveness that keeps us on our spiritual toes. In this sense, honoring change means *welcoming* change—as long as change means real growth. One of the ways to do this is to play with our perception of change, where instead of holding it as a threat, we see it as a passport to adventure. Instead of being "the beginning of the end," we can reacquaint ourselves to change as the beginning of a new chapter in the book of our lives together.

Even as we suggest this expeditionary approach to change, we also want to acknowledge how change always includes an element of loss. This is a tender truth, to be sure. Attachments aren't always due to fearful personalities. Even at the level of soul, we come to cherish the *known* aspects of the people and places we love. Togetherness exists in the flux and seeming complexity of being grateful for where we're at, and also being willing to change. We want things to be stable but life is fluid, and we are all jugglers. Perhaps love is the stable force around which all else revolves.

In all cases, honoring change requires the deeply rooted responsibility that is central to this conversation. In the context of togetherness, change can't be self-serving. Real intimacy values the growth of both people. Cyndi worked with a couple for a period of time that lived together. The woman had a young child from a previous relationship whom she left in the care of her partner when she would travel for work. Now, that's not an unusual scenario, but the issue was that she would take off for two months at a time on a regular basis, and not with her partner's full support. Her growth was self-serving, whereas togetherness is concerned with mutual growth and agreements that work for both partners. To be clear, we are not talking about measured, 50-50 growth. Relationships are rarely balanced in this ideal way. Rather, we're interested in valuing the growth and change of both people as it naturally unfolds.

So when it comes to honoring change, practice an attitude of compassion toward yourself and your partner. Taking time to understand and know your partner more deeply—even if you've been together for many years—is an unexpected key to embracing change. As you look to see what matters to your partner today, what they value today, what dreams and visions for the future they're holding, it's likely that you'll start to welcome their changes. While you look to see how all of that meshes with what you want in your life, you'll also be on their team, cheering them on as they grow and evolve.

To hold their changes as important and rich with meaning, you're naturally being asked by your higher consciousness to do the same for yourself. This is the magic of real intimacy. It is always summoning our most authentic selves.

Change Assessment

On a scale from 1 – 10 (with 1 being very little and 10 being a lot), circle the number that best answers the following question:

To what extent are you welcoming and embracing change in your primary relationship?

1 – 2 – 3 – 4 – 5 – 6 – 7 – 8 – 9 – 10

Contemplation for Growth:
No matter what number you chose for yourself in this moment, what can you do to progress upward on the scale?

Honoring through Acceptance
Just as peace and serenity can attract the quality of love that we desire,

they are also states of being that sustain love. They are native to the together couple, supporting the blossoming of intimacy as they give it room to breath and thrive. And nothing nourishes peace and serenity more than accepting the truth of what *is*. By seeing our partner as *perfectly flawed,* we can accept them without making a demand for change. And in an environment of acceptance, we often see the best in ourselves and others naturally come forward.

It is also important to emphasize that we can't demand change from our partner. We can only discuss consequences if change doesn't occur. When Cyndi works with a client whose partner drinks, she gives them the sobering truth: "You can't make him stop, but you can decide if you stay or not. You hurt both of you if you let yourself be abused."

So, it's also possible that we may see a glaring truth about our partner that we find unacceptable and decide that we don't want to live with them (like Cyndi's example, where they're abusive or addicted and won't ask for help). But there *can* be a peacefulness around that resolve. When we stop making excuses, such as "It's my fault that he hit me," we can see the truth with total clarity. "He hit me again, and that's not alright." Then we can make a decision as to what to do about it from a place of calm honesty.

On a lighter note, Andy's wife Tess accepts that sometimes he doesn't put his things away. And although he has improved in this department, the fact remains that he is still a messy person in certain areas of his life. He accepts this about himself, and so does Tess. For them, it's an area of peace because their priorities are clear. And the truth is, if tidiness were really important to Tess, Andy would try harder to put things away.

Sometimes acceptance comes late in a relationship. Andy worked with a couple whose relationship was riddled with conflict and resentment. The wife lived with cancer for over a decade, and she complained night and day. She complained about the children and constantly corrected and criticized her husband, rarely eking out a kind word to him. Toward the last few months of her life, this woman underwent a metamorphosis. She saw that only love mattered and everything else that she complained about was unimportant. She became whole-heartedly accepting of her husband and kids during her final days. One of the ways she tried to show her love during that fleeting window of time was to urge them to not do what she had done. "Accept each other. Love each other. Don't wait."

Honoring one another through acceptance is a transformation that can happen at any time.

Acceptance Assessment

On a scale from 1 – 10 (with 1 being very little and 10 being a lot), circle the number that best answers the following question:

Think about the traits that your partner has that tend to trigger you or have been a source of concern or conflict for you. To what extent are you accepting of those traits right now?

1 – 2 – 3 – 4 – 5 – 6 – 7 – 8 – 9 – 10

Contemplation for Growth:
No matter what number you chose for yourself in this moment, what can you do to progress upward on the scale?

Honoring Transitions
There are countless books, workshops, retreats, therapies, and love songs all dedicated to the major transition of letting go of a partner who— for some period of time—meant the world to us. Breaking up, letting go, and saying good-bye is not for the faint of heart. When a beloved

dies, the ground permanently shifts beneath the one who lives on in the physical world. And although there are important ways to honor that kind of transition, our focus here pertains specifically to the kind of relationship transition that often leaves at least one of the partners in a wrenching and agonizing internal battle. "Should I stay or should I go?" is the essence of this inner tug-of-war.

Because we have both heard countless clients and friends anguishing over this decision (and sprouting gray hairs and free radicals while they're deliberating), we offer you a laser-focused approach that we're calling "the letting go litmus test"—a direct inquiry that pierces through to the bare essence of things.

When you are contemplating whether or not to end or start a relationship, ask yourself the following two questions and see where the answers naturally lead you:

Do I basically like who this person is?
Is my life better off with them in it?

Transition Assessment

On a scale from 1 – 10 (with 1 being very little and 10 being a lot), circle the number that best answers the following question:

Viewing your relationship through the lens of intimacy and closeness, to what extent are you being honest with yourself about the depth of your togetherness?

1 – 2 – 3 – 4 – 5 – 6 – 7 – 8 – 9 – 10

Contemplation for Growth: No matter what number you chose for yourself in this moment, what can you do to progress upward on the scale?

A Recipe for Joy:
Three Ingredients for Successful Relationships

As you can see, there are many attitudes, beliefs, perspectives, and actions that go into creating successful relationships. In fact, you probably recognize that as an understatement. We have already explored many of those factors in the previous chapters and have a few more priceless ones to share with you up ahead. However, right now we are very deliberately going to ask you to focus your attention on three things—three "ingredients" that mark the pivotal moment in this book. These are three ingredients that will always, when called upon, help you to take your eyes off of the hurt and unfinished business of the past and put them squarely on your love in the present: your man or your woman, your dreams, and the future that Love itself wants you to have. Those three ingredients are:

Forgiveness
Appreciation
Optimism

In short order, we're going to outline for you just how appreciation, optimism, and forgiveness can be some of your best friends in creating a relationship that is successful in ways that exceed your current expectations. Think of each as an *amuse-bouche*, a bite-sized sampling that will offer you big results in sustaining a relationship that calls you to be the person you were born to be.

Forgiveness

At various points along the way, we have talked about the importance of forgiveness. Forgiveness is so vital to living and loving that it's bound to make multiple appearances in a book such as this, just as it appears cyclically in our lives. As in her own relationships, Cyndi works with her clients to help them to be honest about where they are in the cycle of forgiveness. Forgiveness rarely happens in an instant. It's usually a process of making our experiences and feelings more and more conscious. For example, Cyndi's former partner did something at one point that was hurtful to her. When he realized his impact, he felt badly and asked for her forgiveness. Conscious of her own process, Cyndi said she was 75% there. And then she offered him a surprising gift: She told him that she assumed responsibility for getting herself the rest of the way there, and she asked for the time and space she needed to do that.

This depth of honesty let her know what she needed to do to close the gap. What got Cyndi up to the 100% mark was coming to the understanding that forgiveness is really *acceptance*. For a while, she had still been trying to make things different in her mind, temporarily caught in the trap of thinking that you can get a different ending in the reviewing of it. Instead, she accepted what happened and decided to "make something of it"—to learn from it and move forward.

Cyndi's story highlights the importance of not rushing to the kind of forgiveness that's not really forgiveness at all. Don't turn the other cheek prematurely, like Andy's client who "went along to get along." When forgiveness is being called for, honor its cyclical nature by being patient with yourself and your partner. With compassion for both of you, let resentment, bitterness, passive-aggressiveness, and even the urge for revenge melt away. The empathy and love that underlie compassion will help you to find your way to your true feelings. None of us can get away with what Cyndi calls "spiritually bypassing" for too long, where we attempt to skip the emotional work. We have to be committed to doing the excavation in order to change. But as we do this emotional processing, it's encouraging to remember that we don't need to be afraid of what we're feeling. Feelings are perfectly safe! In fact, the only time to fear them is when we deny and ignore them.

Just as Cyndi found out, as you take responsibility for your own forgiveness process, you will usually find that your partner also comes to a place of greater clarity about what they can do to allow healing.

Together you can arrive at an understanding of what will need to change, create an agreement about what needs to change, and then see if there's headway toward it.

Appreciation

Loving Tess helps Andy to keep his priorities straight and his choices clear. He doesn't want to go to his deathbed thinking he could have loved her more, which keeps him deeply in the presence of his appreciation for her and their life together.

Appreciation is really a perspective of *abundance* (which we're going to further explore in the next chapter). Andy looks at what he *does* have with Tess, thanking God daily for the bounty of what is rather than listening to inner chatter about what isn't. Likewise, Cyndi counts her blessings every day, focusing on the love she shares with her partner, with her children, and with her dear friends.

To put appreciation into action involves an understanding of what our partner wants and desires. To make a few useful generalizations, women have a core desire to be cherished, and men have a core desire to be admired for their competence. Cherishing your woman or admiring your man in ways that are specific to them is the pathway for demonstrating your appreciation for them.

Optimism

Do you remember how we said that the heart wants to feel alive? Optimism is one of the best friends of aliveness. What is optimism, really? One of our favorite definitions is that optimism is a belief in the goodness that pervades reality. Forging an alliance with this goodness leads us to expect good things—to look for and find them!

Optimism is spiritually-infused confidence that allows us to anticipate and look forward to things. It says, "Yes, go right ahead! You are hereby released from buying into the weariness of the world and free to enjoy looking forward to things!"

If you want to create a wildly successful relationship, deviate from the routines of life. Plan things that fill you with an anticipatory joy. Schedule things that give you the impetus to complete your responsibilities or projects, while savoring the anticipation of a pleasurable reward at the end. Looking forward to a change of pace, even if it's a simple night out and not having to wash dishes, can fuel optimism and aliveness. It's not only the night out that you benefit from, but also the fun of the anticipation. For couples, when the anticipated event is fun for both partners, looking forward to a change of pace can feel like a breath of fresh air. Don't wait for the scheduled vacation time that you may have coming at some point during the year before breathing in this life-giving air. Breathe it in on a regular basis.

As Andy's father always told him, "You're never to old to listen for the recess bell."

A Reflective Moment

Think about the person that you are closest to, the relationship that is front and center in your life. And then take a moment to reflect on how you can nurture greater optimism and aliveness in the relationship. What could you plan together that would bring the joy of anticipation to life? What would you like to look forward to experiencing together?

CHAPTER 9
SEX: FROM POWER-STRUGGLE TO PASSION

If knowing the truth is sufficient for you, then practice the
art of philosophy. If only living the truth will suffice, then
practice the art of love through your mind,
your emotions, and your body.
–DAVID DEIDA

Sex is a great barometer of intimate relationships. It tells us what kind of weather is brewing both inside and outside the bedroom. It lets us know the atmospheric pressure of what's happening within our hearts and minds. We can rely on sex to be our faithful mirror, always reflecting back to us our beliefs on love, romance, relationships, our bodies, ourselves, and life.

In this chapter, we're encouraging you to take a reading of your own sex life. What's the temperature? Is it warm with passion or chilled by a power struggle with your partner? Or is it a power struggle with your unresolved wounds from the past?

Getting to What's Real: *Uncovering the Blockages to Sex*
Although sharing a life together is a rather complex merging, it can be useful to make certain generalizations, especially when it comes to

addressing the areas that present the biggest challenges. The big three hot button areas that catalyze couples into counseling are sex, money, and the division of labor (which is related to career, home, and parenting). One of the things that we have found to be true in counseling thousands of couples is this: The stated "problem" is almost always a symptom of an underlying issue. If a couple is having little-to-no sex, there are important questions that can help to uncover the true blockages and create real movement.

What are you not talking about with each other?
Is there a secret?
Is there an emotional withhold?
What are the old wounds and fears about intimacy and being loved that could be resolved?

As a couple begins to communicate more openly and honestly—and as they begin to remove mental and emotional obstacles—they rediscover that sex is a natural expression of loving each other. Even for a couple who has been wandering around in a sexual desert for a long time (even years), doubting that they'll ever find an oasis where they can come together again, it can happen! Sex happens naturally when we're emotionally present and vulnerable with each other. And in the pages ahead, we will continue to illuminate various pathways of perception, this time leading to greater sexual openness.

Of course, the amount of sex and the kind of sex that brings the greatest fulfillment and joy varies greatly. Everyone's desire for sex is quite different. One thing that we have found to be true with our clients is that finding satisfaction with each other requires a mutual willingness to move toward the level of desire of our partner. What causes this *movement toward* is a merging of vulnerability, trust, and unbridled affection. For the together couple, this combination is one of the sexiest recipes on earth. When both people feel seen, heard, desired, and cherished, sexual energy (which is an essential aspect of our divine life force) has a chance to ignite.

Emotional Disconnection

Fear of intimacy is one of the greatest obstacles to sexual fulfillment. As obvious as this statement is to most of us, it is essential to address it again with as much courage and honesty as we can draw upon. Whether we're acutely aware of it or only vaguely, without clothes, we are exposed and unprotected. We are open to our partner not only physically but also emotionally, psychologically, and energetically.

From the ego's perspective, our personality is displayed as openly as our bodies. But what is even truer is that in these vulnerable moments, our partner holds our soul as well and our body. Our entire being is laid open to the grace of our partner. Can we trust that they will be kind and caring, treasuring the gifts that we're offering?

In these moments, we are offered a clear choice: Are we willing to give and receive from the deepest place in our hearts? Or will we be guarded or closed off?

Being closed off can run the gamut from saying "no," to listlessly going through the motions, to thinking only of our own pleasure, to being myopically focused on the physical act alone (leaving emotions at the door).

We have dedicated a large portion of this book to addressing the unhealed pain of the past and its aftermath—the unmet needs of the wounded inner child, the emotions that we have repressed or rejected, and the limiting beliefs that we allow to run roughshod over some of the most important parts of our lives. All of this unfinished business is a killer of sexual fulfillment and joy. When we're energetically and psychologically harnessed to the past, it's almost impossible to have great sex—and we mean *really* great sex. The kind of sex that puts you in an ecstatic state of reverberating bliss. Even if it feels rather fleeting, there is a moment where the illusion of separation from your divine source falls away... and it *is* bliss. And it can be more confronting than many of us care to admit.

So we go back to our comfort zone, even if that comfort zone has become more of a dead zone. Out of fear, we go to "sleep" to possibilities that sex wants to awaken in us. And from this sleepy state of consciousness, we make assumptions, decisions, and choices that do very little to bring us closer to our beloved—the partner who was once our lover.

The Problem with Assumptions

Through our thousands of hours of client sessions, as well as through the living of life, we have found that there are two assumptions that so many of us make: 1) how much sex we think other people are having, and 2) how much sex is the "right amount" of sex to be having. These assumptions can wreak havoc in our relationships. We get caught up in what we think romance and sex are supposed to look like. We compare ourselves to others and make choices based on assumptions, rather than asking ourselves, "How does this feel to me? How does this situation impact me? And, by the way, what *is* normal anyway?"

In the movie *Annie Hall*, there is a scene that marvelously illustrates how our ideas of "enough" vary significantly. In their individual therapy sessions, Woody Allen's character (Alvy) and Diane Keaton's character (Annie) complain to their respective doctors about the amount of sex they're having.

Alvy's psychiatrist:
How often do you sleep together?

Alvy:
Hardly ever. Maybe three times a week.

Annie's psychiatrist:
Do you have sex often?

Annie:
Constantly! I'd say three times a week.

The truth is, there is no normal. Couples get to decide this for themselves. In general, what tends to be problematic are the extremes. Cyndi hears from many clients that they're having *zero* sex. Andy has recently been working with a couple who have been married for eight years and have not yet consummated their relationship.

On the flip side, Cyndi had a client who complained about the men she was meeting through an online dating service. She had just come from a first (and only) date with a man who spent the majority of their time together reiterating how he had just come out of a relationship where there was no sex and he really wanted to be sure that he would have *a lot* of sex in his next relationship.

Like Alvy and Annie, it's quite common that one partner desires sex more often than the other. And we want to apologize in advance for furthering the stereotype, but it's usually the man who wants more. Whatever the case may be, the partner who wants sex the least is the one in control of their sex life. This is one of the more obvious ways that the sex becomes a power play rather than a playground of passion.

When Andy is counseling couples, he asks them to try three different replies when one of the partners isn't interested in sex when the other makes their desires known. Imagine yourself being asked to have sex by your partner, while contemplating the impact of these three responses.

One: You can say " yes" anyway.

Two: You can say, "I don't want to have intercourse right now, but how about 'X' as an alternative?"

Three: You can say, "Not now, but how about _____(another time within 24 hours)."

Offering alternatives can help to keep the connection strong between you, whether you're only momentarily out of sync with each other or in the process of discovering the deeper issues that might be in the way.

As we said in the beginning, sex is always a barometer of the overall wellbeing of a relationship, as well as the two individuals who have come together. Cyndi had a client who said that he would have sex with his wife "once in a while" but that he actually wasn't in love with her. He went on to tell Cyndi that he actually didn't even like his wife and that he felt dirty on those rare occasions when he did have sex with her. Cyndi suggested that he stop having sex with his wife altogether and figure out if he wanted to be with her.

The Sexual Chasm

As you can see, the emotional disconnection that happens between couples becomes a widening chasm. Disconnection, distrust, and power struggles come to define their sexual relationship.

Andy saw a couple for a period of time that came to him because they weren't having sex. Keith held a position of authority at his job and Stephanie was a volunteer. Keith changed jobs, taking a new position that paid less and had less prestige. The hot button convergence of money, sex, and power was tearing away at their bond. He felt deflated by his own perceived change of status, while simultaneously feeling angry with Stephanie for not stepping up and getting a paying job to help balance the scales.

Another client of Andy's felt it was his "right" to have sex with his wife whenever he desired. He viewed it as a trade-off since he provided his wife with a comfortable lifestyle (a belief he had unwittingly adopted from his father). Not surprisingly, this trade agreement didn't work for his wife. Rather than feeling like a cherished partner, she told him that she felt like his "whore." The emotional emptiness between them was naturally reflected in the bedroom. As their relationship lacked heart, sex never had a chance to add depth to the relationship.

The Impact of Affairs

As we have explored through this book, all of us need to have the freedom to share the full range of our emotions, and to do this responsibly. Intimacy, closeness, and togetherness depend on it. Couples must be able to share their pain and their fear, as well as their desire and joy. We're naturally going to gravitate to the people and situations that offer emotional connection, and this yearning can sometimes take us down surprising roads. For example, Andy worked with a lesbian couple where one of the women left the relationship and is having an affair with a man. She said that she doesn't like the sex, but he provides the comfort she has been longing for.

Very often, affairs don't start off sexually. They typically start with finding a person we can confide in, especially during stressful periods of time. Jennifer and Brian were another couple that Andy worked with. For a long time, they had shared a loving relationship. But when Jennifer's father became ill and moved in with them, a distance grew between them and their connection was severely tested. While Jennifer was fully consumed with her father's caretaking, Brian felt neglected and threatened to move out. In her anger and despair, Jennifer found someone to talk to who gave her comfort. In a short time, the relationship became sexual.

When Brian found out, he was confronted with difficult choices: How was he going to view his wife now? What was he going to do? He loved her and knew she was going through a difficult time with her father, and yet he felt deeply betrayed and was enraged at her actions. How was he going to integrate both sides? He could continue to act on his anger by punishing her, throwing her out of the house, and bombarding her with hateful phone calls and emails. Or, he could choose to be compassionate, understand his part in the dilemma, and learn new ways to relate. He wrestled with his choices for a long time before choosing the latter.

Brian and Jennifer both came to the realization that all of their choices in the relationship have consequences, good and bad. One of the turning points in their healing came when Jennifer recognized and owned how she had rationalized her decision to get involved with the other man. She had felt justified in seeking solace when her father was slipping away and her husband was missing in action. Admitting to the truth helped Brian in the process of forgiveness.

Cyndi had a client who was married and thinking about having an affair with a co-worker. With no small amount of sincerity, she asked Cyndi, "Do you think that's an okay thing to do?" In a state of denial, her client desperately wanted someone to give her permission to get her needs met. First of all, Cyndi told her client that she makes no moral judgments about affairs, trusting that people are growing and evolving as they need to. However, she was also very clear to say that it's impossible to have an affair without having it affect the marriage on every level—emotionally, energetically, physically, and spiritually. And no matter how easy it may be to start an affair, it's rarely easy to end one. Cyndi told her, "There is no getting around it: Cheating usually seriously injures a relationship. Know that you are playing with fire."

On the Other Side of Hurt

Another client of Cyndi's was married to a man whom she deeply loved. However, in the ten years that they had been together, Marcy had had sex with her previous husband on four different occasions. She felt torn apart inside by her actions, but she also recognized that she was heartbroken by the idea of completely disconnecting with her ex. She really didn't think she could let him go emotionally, and so she was contemplating leaving her current husband.

Eventually, Marcy told her husband what she had done, which was the catalyst for both of them working with Cyndi to help them heal the rift between them. In addition to suggesting that they enroll in a renowned sexuality program at their local university, Cyndi worked with Marcy to identify the "either/or" wall that sex had become to her and her ex-husband. Standing on one side of the wall meant that having sex with him once every few years would keep them "bonded" together. On the other side of the wall, he was gone. That side of the wall was bleak and devastating to Marcy. Helping her to see that the solution could be less painful and more loving, Cyndi said, "Dissolve the wall and discover how you can love each other without sex in the middle." Although Marcy was unwilling to say goodbye to her ex-husband, she didn't really want to have sex with him and obliterate her marriage. Creating new energetic boundaries with him was the beginning of the healing for everyone involved.

One more memorable client of Andy's was Robert, a man who had spent years having sex randomly and with many different partners. Even when he would settle for a while into a relationship, in his words, "sex was just screwing." When Robert started working with Andy, he was in a relationship with Sheila, a woman he had cheated on several times. It had quickly become a pattern for them: He would cheat. She would find out. They would argue. She would be in emotional pain. And eventually things would calm down for a while, until the next incident. But then an amazing metamorphosis took place: Robert actually got tired of hurting Sheila. As he gradually discovered his true feelings for her, he felt remorseful about cheating and finally stopped. Now Robert enjoys having sex with her and has made the distinction between sex and making love.

When there's been a breach of trust, it can take an inordinate amount of time to have it return, and it often takes much longer than we think it will. One of the little-known reasons for this is the energetic cords that form between people when they have sex.

It's difficult to experience the emotional vulnerability, honesty, and presence that are necessary for forgiveness and healing when we're energetically attached to the past.

When we have sex with people, we "take on" or absorb each other's energies. These energies are an amalgamation of our current emotional states, undigested past sexual experiences, unresolved emotions related to past lovers, and much more. That's a lot to carry around! In fact, it can feel so burdensome that sometimes we have sex in order to shake off the energetic weight and leave the old energy with our lover.

There are many ways to cut the cords stemming from the past, but one very simple way that you can put to use right away is this:

Gently close your eyes and take a deep breath, sending radiant oxygen all the way down to the tips of your toes.

Allow yourself to sense or see the energetic cords stemming from your past sexual experiences, whether from last week or thirty years ago. You don't need to see the cords in great detail; it's enough to simply sense their existence.

Invoke spirit in a way that is personal, comforting, and uplifting to you— whether it's inviting your Guardian Angel, your Higher Self, your Higher

Power, God, or any other form of Love. Ask this Higher Power to help you to release the cords now and let the past take care of itself.

Know that you don't have to remember the specific experiences, places, or faces. For now, simply trust the process and have faith that the Source of all creation will support you in being completely free of the past. All you need to do is ask...

Into the Present

Whether straight or gay, there are thoughts, feelings, and behaviors that tend to fall on either end of the spectrum of masculine and feminine energies. For the sake of simplicity, we're referring to them here as differences between men and women. For example, women are afraid that a man will have an affair and fall in love. Men are more afraid that a woman will enjoy sex with another man than form an emotional connection. When having an argument, men like to make–up and reconnect by having sex. They feel closer by having sex. On the other hand, women need to feel close first, and then celebrate that closeness with sex.

Speaking specifically about men and women, we are wired differently. Bridging the gender gap takes patience and a willingness to cultivate greater sensitivity, awareness, and empathy for each other. We need to do more than enhance our relationship with positive interactions. We must also refrain from criticism, blame, and shame. Doing the latter builds a foundation of safety and trust where both people feel safe to express their honest thoughts and feelings.

As evidenced by the stories above, when we don't feel safe and loved, we will eventually either find someone else to connect with or retreat into loneliness and resentment—or sometimes both.

Forgiveness and understanding helps us to release old pain and prepare us for experiencing true fidelity. We're not talking about the "white-knuckling" kind of fidelity, where we try like crazy not to cheat or wait with high expectations to be cheated on, but a fidelity that is alive and vibrant.

What does a broader definition of fidelity include? We would suggest that it starts from the inside out. First ask yourself, "Do I have trust, faith, and confidence in myself? Am I loyal to my own heart?" When we don't trust our partner, we will discover that there is somewhere within the privacy of our own inner world where we don't trust ourselves. That doesn't mean that our partner isn't fully responsible for their own actions and choices; they are indeed. But the seat of our power lies on the inside—with the willingness to look within and know ourselves.

Inherent in both fidelity and sex is the need for boundaries and an understanding of what Cyndi refers to as the "big choices" that determine those boundaries. If you want to create life-affirming boundaries—boundaries that support the evolution of your heart and soul—then the key to identifying and creating these boundaries is quite simple: *let love be the filter.*

Love will tell us when to have sex; how to have sex; where to have sex, and with whom. Love can be trusted. And no matter what we have been through in the past, we can be drawn directly in the present moment by the power of love. It allows you to look into the eyes of your lover and say, "I am here with you. I am present. I am open."

Sexual Enlightenment

As we are sure you have noticed, in our society we put a great deal of attention on orgasm instead of the fuller experience of sex—the process, if you will. We look to the climactic peak of the mountain rather than enjoying the excursion we take to get there. Similarly, we almost always think of sex as being intercourse.

Of course, intercourse and orgasms are some of the great gifts of inhabiting a human body, intensely beautiful in the ways they allow us

174

to merge with each other and even touch the Infinite. However, as we bring this chapter to a close, we want to leave you with a new idea of sex—one that doesn't need to take the place of what you already know about sex and value about it. Instead, we want to offer you a perspective that you can add to everything you already love about sex; an idea that applies whether you are currently single, dating, or in a monogamous relationship.

Our invitation to you is to awaken deep affection for yourself,
your lover, and your life.

As an expression of intimacy, sex can be anything that heightens your awareness, beckons your soul, and arouses your body and spirit. In this regard, affection is an underestimated force for arousing the fullness of a human being.

Of course, we're not referring to the sugary-sweet version of affection. We're referring to an affection that arises spontaneously and powerfully, an affection that starts as a deep recognition of the gift that appears before you when you are standing in the mirror, either alone or with your partner.

This is an affection that hones the passion of your spirit and compassion of your soul to a fine focal point, culminating in a touch, a soft whisper, a look in the eyes of the person you love. Physically, affection can be shown in countless ways, from holding each other, stroking each other's backs, kissing, touching your lover's hand—any touch that transmits the excitement, acceptance, and receptivity that you wish to convey.

Energetically, deep affection is a sensuous aliveness. It springs forth naturally out of the present moment, like a beautiful wave bringing a message from your heart onto the shore of your lover. Unabashedly, affection gently washes over both of you with its gratitude, wonderment, and delight at having the opportunity to touch another and be touched.

A Reflective Moment

Take a moment to be still and allow yourself a mini meditation. Breathing in and out, feel the sensations and energy in your body right now. Notice the vibration and aliveness of your being. Observing your sensual and sexual energy through the eyes of the divine within you, what would that part of you like to say right now?

CORNERSTONE IV
Togetherness with the Divine

THE FOURTH CORNERSTONE of togetherness is
the relationship you have with the Divine, by whatever
name you use to refer to the invisible life force that holds
and sustains life. For you, your reference point might
be Higher Power, Source, or God. Within the final three
chapters that comprise Part IV, we are shining a light
on the source of the love that moves in and through us.
Along the way, we will guide you in examining the roots
of true prosperity in relationships (a conversation that
includes a refreshing perspective on money); discovering
the magnificent power of kindness in loving one another;
understanding how deep friendship and community calls
you forward to express your highest potential as a human
being; and deepening the bond between you and spirit.
To send you on your way feeling empowered and inspired,
we will leave you with a blueprint for what we call The
Continual Courtship, the simple and uplifting guidelines
for treating each other as the embodiment of the divine.
Follow these recommendations and prepare for a sacred
love affair that knows no end.

CHAPTER 10
RELATIONSHIP PROSPERITY

When you realize there is nothing lacking,
the whole world belongs to you.
–LAO TZU

How often has money been a source of stress and angst in your primary relationship? If you're like most of us, there have been memorably difficult moments when you would swear that money existed to test the viability of your relationship and the resilience of your love.

As you can probably tell, we empathize.

It is true that money plays a *huge* role in our lives. It's also true that few of us are immune to the fears and power struggles that can arise in relationship to money and material possessions. But the way we deal with money—how we earn it, spend it, lose it, regain it, and feel about it—is really an outer reflection of our inner bank account.

So, as important a topic as money is, this chapter is not about how to jointly manage your finances or how to best communicate when the financial heat is on—not directly anyway. Instead, we want to invite you into a deep conversation with us where we will explore the deeper meaning of prosperity and the real source of wealth.

Although we are primarily focusing on the prosperity and abundance that is sourced from within, we would also like to address *money*—the currency that affects our lives in such an intimate way on a daily basis.

Generally speaking, for men, money is power. For women, money is safety.

When money is in short supply, men tend to feel emasculated, and women tend to feel anxious and worried. For either gender, money concerns cause stress, erode confidence, and deplete our ability to experience closeness, trust, and pleasure with one another. It's true that money is one of the top three issues that drive couples to seek the help of therapists, counselors, and coaches.

One of the single most important pieces of advice we can give you when it comes to money is to KEEP TALKING. Don't allow resentments and misunderstandings to build up between you. Toward that end, here are two perspectives and practices that you can put to use right away:

Remember that you are on the same team! So keep talking until you find solutions to money situations that will work for both of you. Also, remember that it's important to stretch in your partner's direction (as well as for them to stretch in your direction). For example, if you're trying to decide whether or not to spend money on something, you could ask your partner: "Is there anything we could do that would help you to be comfortable with *not* spending that money?" Or, "Is there anything we could do that would help you to be comfortable *with* spending that money?"

179

Valuing your combined resources. Money is often seen as more important than other resources. However, to cultivate a healthy, happy dialogue with your partner related to money, it's essential to hold money in a larger context—where you are *equally* valuing the other splendid resources that you and your partner share with each other. Imagine what would be possible if you and your beloved were willing to see each of the following resources as equally valuable: *earning a salary; caring for the children; cleaning the house or apartment; doing yard work; maintaining vehicles; doing laundry; running miscellaneous errands and shuttling children to events; shopping for groceries and household items; cooking meals; organizing parties, celebrations, and family gatherings; and handling accounting, including bill paying and maintaining important records.* Looking at the larger picture of your lives together, decide how you would like to blend and balance your resources and responsibilities.

As we continue to reveal perceptions and choices that are essential for helping both individuals and couples to flourish at the deepest level, our intention is to expand your ideas of how prosperity and abundance are manifested in the context of a successful and healthy relationship. And perhaps most surprising of all will be the discovery of kindness as the true currency of the together relationship.

Welcoming Pure Existence

We (Cyndi and Andy) devote time each day to tending to our own intimate relationships and supporting our clients to do the same. What we have discovered over time are some of our "trade secrets" for how to achieve spiritual abundance—where there is an overflowing fullness of love in the relationship, and how to create emotional and energetic prosperity—where the hearts of both partners are thriving.

What does prosperity and abundance mean to you?

What would your life look like if you were all of a sudden "abundant?"

If your bills were all current, your debts paid off, and your bank account was brimming with abundant cash, how do you imagine you would feel?

If opportunities for advancement in your professional field were to suddenly increase, how do you imagine you would feel?

Now for the big question:

If the man or woman at your side showed you in no uncertain terms how deeply they love you, melting away any doubt, how do you imagine you would feel?

There is great excitement linked with acquiring things and achieving goals, even with having a relationship. Just owning stuff and making things happen, however, doesn't create the sense of abundance we're really looking for. Simply being in a relationship doesn't necessarily lead to a feeling of wholeness either.

When we get down to it, when it comes to money or relationships, we not only want to feel peaceful—we want to *be* at peace. We want to feel rested, relaxed, and open to life. We want to feel as we would in a postcard setting, relaxing on a tropical beach, slathered in sunscreen, and holding a great book in one hand and a piña colada in the other. We long for that type of peace, the peace of simplicity and tranquility. We yearn for the peace of a vacation, like what we feel in those moments when we complete our projects or chores and are afforded our own time.

Folk stories and fairy tales of every culture reflect the goal of relationship peace. Do you remember what happens with Snow White and her prince or the Frog and the Princess? As their stories come to a satisfying conclusion, there is a peacefulness surrounding the protagonist and their beloved. There is shared elation as they revel in the triumph of good and the realization of their dreams. But there is an even subtler enchantment as well. There is a joyous calm that pervades, a serenity that both surrounds the couple and extends beyond them.

When we dip below the roiling waves of our busy and sometimes worried minds, we too can sink into this place of inner peace and share it with others. There is perhaps nothing more deeply bonding than this. When we're present to our divine inner connection, there is a generosity of spirit, a kindness that ripples outward. In our closest relationships, when we are at peace with ourselves, we exude that feeling, extending it to our partner and to the world.

The longing to bask in this peace and kindness is one of the reasons that so many people are drawn to spiritually awakened teachers. If you have ever stepped into a room with a guru, you have felt this peace spiritually but also physically. You have sensed an inner joy that is palpable.

Gurus are not naïve to the injustices and pain of the world. They are aware of suffering; they have felt it themselves. Their focus, however, is on the present moment, anchored by a wonderment that includes *all* of life's manifestations. In this inclusiveness, they continually celebrate the miracle of life as it happens. Their aura of appreciation pulsates with a sense of wellness and equanimity, and we find ourselves attracted to an astonishing state of being: where there is no inner or outer battle going on and no greater desire than the desire for what *is*.

This is an example of true inner wealth, a whole-hearted embrace of the abundance that simply is. It describes the opulence of life that many of us are blind to...until a day comes that opens our eyes. Maybe a tragedy pries us open or a delicate grace softly awakens us, but in any case, we discover that we cannot logically account for the exquisite blessings of the love we have shared in our lives. And even if we haven't yet had the one great romantic love that we've been waiting for, there is at least one person in this world—a dear friend, a grandparent, a teacher, a guardian angel in physical form—who has loved us dearly.

Each of us has mattered to someone. And that is a wealth that no banking system can track.

Each of us has the capacity to recognize and welcome the miracle of life, but sometimes life itself gets in the way. We're more apt to get in touch with the truth of abundance when we take a momentary breather from our trials and tribulations. In these quiet times we notice that our existence, our life, is the true miracle. If we are alive, if we are able to embrace our existence, we *are* abundant.

Once we're able to clearly recognize this ever-present abundance, we let down our guard. We soften. We stop warring internally. We question the need to be right all the time. We lose the drive to be right, to have more, to get on top, or to find something (or someone) better. We find that we actually do have enough time to stop and smell the roses, and we can even do it *together*. As we notice that life is constantly generous, we become more generous in return.

What does true prosperity and abundance look like in the together relationship? And what fosters it? Most notably, peaceful abundance is felt when we accept our partner for who they are and let go of who we want them to be. This does not mean that we have to agree with everything they do or say. Peacefulness is a matter of perspective that doesn't require perfection. When we understand that people are not here to guarantee our happiness now or in the future, we're able to see them from a new vantage point. Deep peace—the kind that passes all understanding—comes from knowing that we all come from the Source. This understanding is the source of spiritual empathy. We're all sewn from the same cloth, and we are all trying to work our way through this world the best way we know how.

Problems occur when we try to make our partner into someone they are not. It's useful to admit that we sometimes want them to adapt and change to whatever extent suits us and fills our needs and desires. Sometimes we try to make them into a "better" person, but this never really works out well for them or for us. However, there is an alternate method of engagement that is infinitely more fulfilling. If we are willing to pay attention and notice the amazing life story being lived by our partner, we touch what the gurus experience—and begin to offer what they offer. We embody the joy and peacefulness that we see written in the fairy tale endings.

A fascinating paradox here is that in welcoming the purity of existence, we can embrace even the belief in deprivation. All is welcome. This doesn't mean that we necessarily like everything that happens—like disasters, injustices, or misfortune. Rather, we exude a warmth that says, "I am open to receiving life as it is. Rather than fighting with reality, I use love as the filter for my experience, and I trust my heart to put everything in perspective." In the glow of this sincere welcome, deprivation, scarcity, and the fear that gives birth to them are all comforted and often healed at the hearth of loving acceptance.

When we feel grateful for the miracle of existence, we also discover a new way to gauge our successes and our failures. Although we're conditioned to measure success by comparing ourselves to others, quantifying who has "more or better," we now assess our wealth by how we *feel* about ourselves, not how "the Joneses" might perceive us.

Gratitude is a winning lottery ticket all by itself. We win each time we breathe in love and breathe out a whisper of "Thank you, God. Thank you for all the care, beauty, and light in my life."

Knowing Acts of Loving-Kindness

How many times have you stopped at a traffic light and seen a bumper sticker on the car in front of you that says: *Practice random acts of kindness*? It's a potent invitation that, once we get past any eye-rolling cynicism, can be used for real inspiration. We can take that car-bumper proverb and turn it into relationship gold.

For several years, Andy has been practicing, and advocating, what he refers to as "knowing acts of loving-kindness." Rather than making random acts, he makes purposeful and personal acts—actions that are infused with attentive love. As a practice, this type of giving promotes and deepens intimacy. In the together relationship, these thoughtful behaviors aid you in discovering what appeals to your partner as a unique individual. You are now able to understand what pleases them and give them what *they* want, not what *you* want.

Performing knowing acts of loving-kindness doesn't need to be complicated. There are simple ways that we can feed the soul of a relationship. For example, Andy makes coffee for Tess every morning although he doesn't drink coffee. And Tess waits to have dinner with Andy every night, even though he often gets home late. They make these choices not out of obligation, but to bring pleasure to one another and to reinforce the closeness of their bond.

We've only to add to the pleasure of our partner's day to give the type of love that will be remembered and treasured. When both people in a relationship give and receive this way, we can't help but become more and more intimate and prosperous. This is a quality of prosperity that can't be quantified. This is love in abundance.

Standing on the Sacred Ground of Kindness
As you have noticed throughout this book, kindness is an elemental thread in the tapestry of togetherness. When we talk about kindness, we're not referring to a saccharine niceness but something of far greater substance. Kindness is caring for another from a wellspring of authentic emotional generosity. It involves considering what matters to another when making choices that affect them. In the together relationship, kindness is a caring that honors the dignity and grace of our partner.

With their clients and within their own relationships, Cyndi and Andy have discovered that kindness is one of the greatest forces for good in relationships. Nowhere is this more the case than when we run into misunderstandings, conflict, and hurt within our relationships.

Whether the conflict is large or small, when an issue erupts between two people, kindness has a surprising potency for restoring balance. It is the spiritual solution with a distinct practicality to it. Kindness says, "You matter more than this conflict. You matter more than who is right and who is wrong. So, from that playing field, what are we going to do to make this work?" Kindness also says, "I know you; I know what will make you feel good, and I'm going to do that."

Cyndi and her ex-husband were a few years into their divorce when they arrived at a crossroads. They were contemplating whether it was time to deepen their commitment to kindness or follow the world's curriculum and be embittered "exes." Both decided to serve each other's highest evolution. After wrestling for a short time with the significance of the decisions that were in front of them, they made a breathtaking choice together to try a fresh approach and actually LIKE each other. As Cyndi described it, "We saw that we could stand on the ground of kindness together, deeply befriending one another. That's the ground of love and care where God's will unfolds; where all of the 'what should we do?' questions are divinely answered."

In chapter 4, we wrote about the powerful energetic boundary that kindness can provide in a relationship. At first glance, this may seem like an oxymoron, as if kindness should only dissolve the lines that separate us rather than establish them. But we're not talking about the average boundary here. We're talking about a boundary that provides a meeting point, not a barricade. On the shore of kindness, we honor the substance, meaning, and intrinsic value of one another.

In the most basic terms, when kindness is an energetic boundary in your relationship, you know that your partner is more than someone to have sex with, to share meals with, to "bounce things off of," or to pay for half of the household expenses. In the midst of even the most routine day or mundane task, kindness reminds you that your partner is an embodiment of the divine. And although kindness would never ask you to abandon yourself, kindness does encourage moments when the focus is less about you and more about them.

Do you remember the acorn and the oak tree? We began our journey describing how the acorn is an intimate expression of the mighty tree, just as togetherness is an intimate expression of love's immensity. Similarly, kindness is a nourishing droplet arising from the ocean of compassion. Kindness focuses and directs compassion in ways that are personal and particular to the beloved spouse, partner, or friend who is the recipient of your loving attention. A kind thought that may never be spoken aloud, a knowing look, an arm wrapped around a shoulder to bring assurance in a moment of uncertainty—these are just a few simple examples of the kindnesses that bring soulfulness to our daily interactions.

When Leaving Is an Act of Kindness

Cyndi once had a client who had been repeatedly beaten by her alcoholic husband. And it didn't stop with her, either; he also beat their children. Being devoutly religious, her client went to her priest for guidance and was advised not to leave because "it's a sin to leave a marriage."

Cyndi asked this lovely yet wounded woman why she felt that she needed to stay in this abusive marriage. Her client told her that she felt guilty for smoking cigarettes. She believed that smoking was a sin. And because she believed that she already had this one big strike against her, she believed that if she left her husband on top of her "smoking sin," God would surely punish her.

Using a bit of irreverent humor to help her client open her eyes and break free, Cyndi said, "Go home, light two cigarettes, and ask God to smoke one with you!" It was also a playful way for Cyndi to assure her client that God wasn't holding the smoking against her. The only punisher to get away from was her husband. Cyndi's primary aim was to communicate to her client that there could be a path out of her dismal marriage and the self-abandonment that it required of her. There could be a much softer approach to changing a very hard situation. By the way, she did leave her husband and is healing her heart and her children's hearts.

Although Cyndi's client offers an extreme example, too many of us put ourselves through senseless and protracted bouts of pain and suffering in our relationships. If you are considering whether to leave a relationship, or if you come to that point in the future, claim it as a grand opportunity to practice being kind to yourself. First of all, before making any decisions, give yourself permission to take the time you need to build yourself up and take care of yourself. Give yourself the time to look within and contemplate questions such as, "Am I assuming responsibility for issues that are not my own?" Or, "Am I leaving because I can't achieve intimacy here, or because I'm scared of intimacy?

Letting go of a relationship is rarely a black and white decision. The fear of failure and loss can create a lot of confusion that makes a difficult process even harder. And in some cases, it can take months and even years to know what's best for you. This is the time to show yourself the kindness that always brings the light of clarity with it.

Andy's client Jason had dated a woman who was on the fast-track to getting married, having a big house with the picket fence, and starting a family. She had the next 30 years all worked out! Jason, on the other hand, was passionate about his new line of work, and he also wanted to devote more time to studying with a various spiritual teachers to learn more about his own gifts. He wasn't in any way ready to embrace what his girlfriend wanted. But, he cared very deeply for her. After much deliberation, he decided that as an act of kindness, he must tell her how he truly felt. He felt that they both deserved to live their deepest truth and to be free to live their lives accordingly. So, Jason finally broke up with her, telling her that he wanted her to be happy to pursue her dream. They both flourished from standing on this ground of kindness, which meant walking away from each other. Jason is now happily married with one child. And his former partner is married and has two children. Many have prospered from both their coming together and their coming apart.

Cherishing Our Losses
When someone we love dies, the ground beneath us is shaken and fractured. This is when we most require the fierce strength that sacred kindness can provide. This is when we'll most feel it when it's offered.

One of Cyndi's friends was feeling acute pain over the loss of his mother. She could feel that he was suffering despite the " stiff upper lip" credo that controlled his moods. Cyndi encouraged him to talk about all of it—the devastation of the loss, a few regrets he was harboring, the things he still wanted to say to his mom, and some of the memories of her that he treasured. As partners in love or friendship, we can help each other through the pain and fear that comes with loss, and we can encourage one another to grow from it.

As the poet and mystic Kahlil Gibran wrote, "When you are sorrowful look again in your heart, and you shall see that in truth, you are weeping for that which has been your delight.

A Reflective Moment

Taking a moment to be still and quiet, notice where in your life you feel most prosperous. In what part of your life are you enjoying an abundance of riches — whether it's an abundance of opportunities, resources, people, love, or some other experience of plentitude? Notice how it feels to hold this abundance in your awareness.

CHAPTER 11
MIRRORS OF LOVE: COMMUNITY
AS A PATH TO WHOLENESS

*Real friendship or love is not manufactured or achieved by
an act of will or intention...in the moment of friendship,
two souls suddenly recognize each other.*
–JOHN O'DONOHUE

Despite the "you and me against the world" approach that some couples take, we'll never be happy hiding ourselves away in protective isolation. In a world shared by seven billion people, it's just not feasible to close our eyes to one another. We are a vast community of women, men, children, and nature—expressions of spirit in physical form. And no matter how many borders we draw, walls we build, or pass codes we install, the truth is that we are meant to be here *together*.

Community means different things to different people. Not everyone wants a big community. To Andy, community means "a simple love affair with a few good friends"—culminating during the warm months with Sunday softball. Tess enjoys a larger group of friends, so Andy stretches sometimes beyond his community comfort zone to share time with them.

For Cyndi, community is both a very intimate part of her life (remember the sister-friends?) and yet a multifaceted part, too. In addition to her close friends and confidants, her extended community is a collage of other moms, sports coaches, colleagues in the world of transformational writers and teachers, neighbors, the people at her favorite coffee shop, at the post office, and beyond.

Community serves many purposes, including the enjoyment of sharing an affinity with a group of people, taking pleasure in the sharing of interests, ideas, passions, resources, and opportunities. However, in this brief chapter, we want to delve right into the depths of what community offers us.

We're going to begin with a little walk down a yellow brick road and explore how our circles of friends and loved ones are helping us to evolve from the many back to the One.

The Mirrors of Oz

In *The Wizard of Oz*, Dorothy's journey with the friends she meets along the yellow brick road exemplifies one of the great gifts we give to each other as a collective human family. It shows how we mirror for each other the qualities, attributes, and traits that we have forgotten we possess. Our own beliefs—and our ability to believe in others—often form the bridge that others need to regain access to wholeness.

When Dorothy first meets the Scarecrow, he is stuck hanging life-lessly on his pole. Dorothy helps free the Scarecrow and asks him to join her on her journey. Because of her interest and caring, he begins to come alive. Seeing this as an opportunity to search for the brain he believes he's lacking, he sets off down the yellow brick road of promise with Dorothy.

When Dorothy and the Scarecrow first meet the Tin Man, he is a rusty patchwork of tin that can't even move. With the help of some oil (a dose of kindness) and a promise to search for a heart, he joins the duo. As Dorothy and the Scarecrow express a sincere interest in the Tin Man—as they widen the circle of belonging—he too is inspired to join them on their adventure. When the threesome finally meet up with the Lion, they find someone who is alone, isolated, and afraid of everything. Now the Lion is drawn into the circle of friendship and shared adventure. Naturally, it took some persistence to encourage the Lion to come along, as courage was the very characteristic he was certain he didn't have.

Dorothy's new friends believed that she and the Wizard could help them find what they were certain they lacked. But no one else had the power to restore these qualities because they were already alive within them! Dorothy and the Wizard provided that bridge of belief where they could rediscover what they had never really lost—only forgotten for a while.

The brain, heart, and courage they were looking for represented more than thinking, feeling, and will alone. The Scarecrow wanted to reclaim the power of personal choice that thinking allows. The Tin Man wanted access to his intuitive heart again. And he wanted to love and be loved. For the Lion, finding his courage would reconnect him with his inherent power. He was tired of cowering in the corner and wanted to find the strength needed to take action, to face life head-on. In their quests, they were unlikely yogis on the path to self-realization—in search of knowledge, devotion, and meaningful action.

Of course, it wasn't only Scarecrow, Tin Man, and the Lion who were in need of guidance, support, and love. Dorothy and even the Wizard of Oz himself had their own inner conflicts and fears. By coming together, they each found the hope that propelled them forward. Their sense of community, albeit a bit unusual, gave them the strength to persevere in a manner they might not have found individually.

This beloved cast of characters mirrored for each other what was already inside each of them. This is the beauty of relationship. When we see ourselves reflected in our friends' eyes, when we let our guard down even a little bit, we can see things about ourselves that we previously had only hoped were true. This validation helps to bring us alive in ways that we often don't perceive on our own. We're designed to shine a light for one another when we get lost in darkness, the latter caused by forgetting who we really are.

As for Dorothy and her friends, their story is a mirror for each of us, reflecting the wholeness and freedom of being that we sometimes forget.

Preparation for Enlightenment

Needless to say, we don't always like what we see in the mirror that others provide for us. However, noticing our internal reactions to others—to our mother, brother, co-worker, boss, child, neighbor, friend, or anyone else—provides endless opportunities for growth. Others help us to see what we believe about ourselves and about life. The crucial distinction in figuring out what someone is mirroring back to us is this: Other people aren't reflecting back to us our actual measure of value or worth; they're reflecting back what we *believe* to be true about our value and worth.

Here we are on this breathtaking planet together. We are all seeking to return home, not only to heaven, but to the truth of our being. And yet so much of the time we concentrate on what is "wrong" with others or ourselves. What if we were to instead acknowledge that we are more alike than different? And that we are more "good" than "bad", no matter how miserable we sometimes feel or even act?

What if we were to go further and embrace ALL feelings and realities, good and bad, as stair-steps into personal enlightenment? Every teeter-totter we experience prepares and polishes us for awakening into love.

And while we are here to advance our own soul, we are also here to advance the souls of others. We are meant to take the cumulative learning we have gathered (in this lifetime and before) and use that understanding to help move others along as well as ourselves. Humankind is supposed to move upward together en masse. While each of us has

194

our own unique purpose to fulfill and enjoy, we also share a collective purpose. We are all in the world together working toward the same "goal"—togetherness with the divine.

This awareness is an antidote to the dog-eat-dog thinking of the world. All of us, together right now, are the culmination of many generations that point in the same direction—away from the pain of separation and into the light of belonging. By remembering that we are all woven from the same cloth, no matter how cynical we can be at times, we smooth out the ruffled edges of our minds. Recognizing and remembering our sacred commonality is another path to deep peace and serenity.

Whether you're in an intimate love relationship now or longing for the arrival of your beloved, it's vital to tend to the garden of your community. When we're connected to our community, we feel uplifted by the experience of contributing to one another. We revel in our enjoyment of the journey together and can bring that joy back to the love we share at home. And when we feel loved at home, we bring that love outward into the world as a blessing to all.

Again, the size of a community doesn't matter in and of itself. It could be a community of three friends or fifty, but what does matter is the way that our community nourishes us and calls us forward to express our highest potential and our deepest love. Real community brings us closer to the entirety of our human family.

What happens when our circle of loved ones, friends, colleagues, and collaborators inspires us to be more involved with the world? Our relationship expands and evolves. Our personal intimacy grows. We don't lose by supporting our partner's participation in their community. We benefit.

In long-term relationships, we often enjoy a shared community. No matter how separate or overlapping our circles are, we provide our partner with a priceless gift when we encourage them to strengthen, deepen, and take great pleasure in the bonds they share with others.

Of course we also need to involve ourselves deeply in our own community of love and support. It's interesting to see how so many of us will take out insurance policies on our homes, our cars, and our bodies, all for the very legitimate purpose of having safety and security. But we will often neglect the "safe house" that community provides our soul. Being involved with others in meaningful and enriching ways offers psychological, emotional, and spiritual safety that can't be bought with monthly payments.

Of course we're not referring to the kind of safety that guarantees that nothing painful or difficult will happen in our lives. Life doesn't hand us these guarantees. Instead, we're referring to a kind of ineffable safety and security that is felt when we look into each other's eyes and see the indestructible face of God looking back—when we deeply see and know each other as spirit courageously inhabiting a human life.

There is an eternality in friendship that is one of the sweetest parts of living a human life. And within our circles of belonging there are great undiscovered possibilities waiting to be found. There is so much to do together—to create, to explore, to laugh about, to plan for. And there is much to simply witness together, sometimes without uttering a word but just noticing some small delight or a shared moment of awe.

Bruce Springsteen's moving eulogy for his dear friend and longtime band mate Clarence Clemons was made available on the *Rollingstone* website. In it, Springsteen poured his soul into describing their friendship—a friendship they shared within a community of musicians and fans that has positively impacted millions of people around the world. For four decades they created community through music, and helped move each other closer to the source, further up the road of enlightenment.

I'm no mystic, but the undertow, the mystery and power of Clarence and my friendship leads me to believe we must have stood together in other, older times, along other rivers, in other cities, in other fields, doing our modest version of god's work… work that's still unfinished. So I won't say goodbye to my brother, I'll simply say, see you in the next life, further on up the road, where we will once again pick up that work, and get it done.

At the very heart of it, community is standing together—here, now, and forever. Take care of your community, and let your community take care of you. Let it strengthen you, empower you, and inspire you to love. Let it return you to your wholeness, which is the beautiful truth at the center of your being.

A Reflective Moment

Think about your community for a moment, seeing the faces of the people that encircle you. As you breathe in, sense the gratitude that you naturally feel for them. What one thing you could do within the next 24 hours to express your appreciation for your community?

CHAPTER 12
DANCING WITH THE DIVINE

To love another person is to see the face of God.
– FROM *LES MISERABLES*

As you arrive at the final chapter of this book, we invite you to enter into it as if entering a meditation hall. This is a calming place to contemplate the sanctuary of love in your life; it is fragrant with incense and the sweetness of your hopes, dreams, and desires.

Can you hear the meditation bell being gently rung by the old and luminous teacher? He is calling his students into deep awareness of the present, asking questions that can serve to awaken all of us from passing through life on autopilot.

How do you want to feel at the end of your life? When you take your last breath, will you feel that you have fulfilled your deepest purpose? Will you feel joyful about the love you have given and received?

The reason to consider how we want to feel at the end of our lives is to inform and inspire the way we're choosing to live in the present. Contemplating how we want to feel *then* can affect the priorities we set for ourselves and our relationships right *now*.

In the together relationship, fast-forwarding in our minds to the end of our lives together in the physical realm can inspire us to contemplate and answer important questions, such as:

What do we want our relationship to be *about*?

What is the vision we have for our relationship in the future?

And what is here right now; what is the substance of "us"?

The relationship is its own entity that needs to be nourished as such. It has to be about the two of you before anything outside, even children. In order to build a foundation that is strong enough to hold the weight of sharing children, careers, finances, family, friends, and even causes, it's important to have a shared vision.

Dynamic and evolving, this shared vision doesn't get created or sustained by default. It requires time and attention and the intentional exploration of what matters to you, what holds meaning for you, what inspires you, and what calls you as a couple to live *into* your potential—individually and together.

For each of us, deciding what we want our relationships to be about happens within the context of our day-to-day togetherness. Many seemingly mundane decisions are made every day: decisions to have sex or not; to talk or not; to spend time together or alone; to sit down together for dinner or grab take-out. And then there are the larger questions, such as how to divide responsibilities and labor; how to make money; who works and who stays home; where to live; to buy or rent; where to spend holidays. And the lists go on.

This is precisely where having a shared vision comes into play. When making those common, everyday decisions, the slide rule needs to be about something much more sublime than simply how to fulfill our proper roles (as wife, husband, mother, father, etc.) or how to do things the way we learned to when we were growing up. Ordinary decisions can be held against the backdrop of an extraordinary miracle that we are here together, that we are spirit in human form and are choosing to share the evolutionary adventure together.

In this sense, the slide rule needs to be about what's *immortal*. Having a vision that shines its guiding light on our lives together helps us to see the obvious connection between our earthly concerns and our heavenly callings.

When Cyndi is working with couples to clarify what their relationship is about, she asks them to practice looking through God's glasses to gain a clearer vision. Many times couples are surprised by what they find when they look at their relationship through the lens of spirit. The light switch of truth gets turned on. A desire to truly know each other replaces persistent projections. Discernment replaces judgment. Exciting possibilities replace unfulfilling fantasies. In an instant of sincerely looking and *seeing* who is in front of us, gratitude arises to heal the blindness that old heartbreak has induced.

When we're able to not only see the many gifts of our togetherness but also be *moved* by them, we become inspired to care for those gifts and allow their meaning to come alive in the *living* of our shared vision.

When Shared Values Aren't Enough

There's an important distinction to be made between having a shared vision and having a shared value system. Problems can arise when a couple has a shared value system but not a shared vision that's based on a bond of intimacy, affection, and respect for each other. A friend of Cyndi's had been married for 24 years and is now divorced. When he and his former wife first met, they were Christians who were deeply involved in their church. And in their youthful naiveté, they were on a mission to "save" Muslims. They had a shared value system based on their fervent religious beliefs but not a shared vision for where love could take them in their relationship. He told Cyndi that out of their 24 years together, they had only been in love for the first six weeks. But within those few short weeks, they had already cemented their relationship into place. They lived unhappily ever-after.

Having common interests and values can add greatly to the enjoyment, pleasure, and comfort that a couple experiences in their relationship, but they alone don't have the power to carry a relationship. Only love does.

But love makes some demands of us.

Love is a creative force that requires much more from us than a list of shared beliefs and preferred activities. Love asks us to notice the emptiness that creeps in when we're looking to another to validate our worth and meaning. It asks us to take a walk of faith—to remember that our worth is inherent and to discover that the meaning of our lives is something we get to choose for ourselves. Love asks us to discover the purpose of our lives as individuals, and if we're in a partnership, to realize that we get to consciously choose our shared purpose.

Embracing the process of discovery is a wonderful antidote to living life by default, to operating from old scripts that usually involve mountains of pain. Love and discovery in concert with one another always asks us to pay attention to the soulful, little details of one another; to notice the patchwork of needs, desires, and delights that are particular to the person we adore. Actively looking for and noticing these things about each other has the amazing effect of nourishing the bond of connection, while simultaneously calming the fears of the parts of ourselves that are afraid of intimacy and prone to worry.

Despite our most inspired intentions, we do go through periods of feeling disconnected from the people and things that matter most to us. Sometimes the disconnection happens suddenly and without warning. And sometimes a chasm grows so gradually that we become accustomed to it, denying or making excuses for the hole that has formed in the middle of our love life.

Letting Your Relationship Evolve

Rosalyn and Ed came to see Andy regarding their 14-year marriage. Both were doctors who met in medical school and both trusted that they would always be able to rely on each other financially. However, neither thought about putting extra attention on the little details of their day-to-day lives together. They were busy. They had their careers, their home, their friends. And then they started to raise a family. Years flew by, and they didn't pay attention to their relationship as a living and breathing force. They were living by default.

When they came to Andy's office for their first visit, Ed was angry because of the lack of sex, and Rosalyn felt completely apathetic about the relationship and therefore uninterested in sex. Her apathy had ever-so-gradually crept in on the heels of disappointment. Despite how we might rationalize it in our minds, when the needs of the heart are ignored for very long, disappointment and pain are bound to settle in.

During one particular session, Rosalyn asked Ed why he made a habit of turning off the CD player when he came into the room. She told him that she enjoyed music, and when he turned it off, she felt angry. This was the first time he had ever heard her voice her feelings about the CD player. "In fact," he retorted, "I never knew until just now that you even liked music."

In fourteen years, he hadn't noticed that his beloved wife enjoyed music. She hadn't shared this with him, and he hadn't been paying attention. It's amazing how distant a couple can become when they take their relationship for granted. Without knowing each other on the inside—without revealing ourselves and without seeking to know the other—intimacy is only an unfulfilled dream. Benign neglect tears at the fabric of a relationship. After awhile, we become business partners or parenting partners rather than devoted lovers and sacred companions.

If you have kids who are still at home, once they go out on their own, the relationship has to stand on its own. What Cyndi and Andy have seen repeatedly with their clients is that waiting until children leave home to connect with one's partner very often ends in divorce. Continuing to know and understand your partner is an investment in your future as a couple. Caring for your relationship and letting it evolve is the fun part. To help you do that, we have created a simple blueprint that will yield remarkable results if you use it as a guide.

Blueprint for The Continual Courtship

Do you simply want to feel comfortable and safe with you partner, or do you want to inspire each other to reach for the heights of your potential?

Do you want to "have a relationship," or do you want to be in love?

*There is no need to settle. One to another, you have the ability to charm the imagination, pursue undiscovered mysteries, and entice the soul to come to the fore. The key to wooing each other in body, mind, and spirit is simple, really. The key is **giving and receiving**.*

When you give to one another through the quality of your attention, you will witness each other blossoming… and right in the midst of any ordinary day. Of course, being able to receive the loving attention offered to each other is just as important.

Soul Directives for the Continual Courtship

Listen: *Listen to each other, taking care to hear what really matters to the other.*

Laugh: *Take great pleasure in each other's company. Look for the humor in the midst of even the most challenging moments, and make having fun a top priority in your togetherness.*

Be curious: Ask about each other's interests, knowing that interests change. As you inquire, look through the eyes of Fascination! Be fascinated by each other, remembering the miracle and wonder that you are both here—together.

Be amazed: At least once a day, look at each other through God's glasses—be amazed, be moved, be surprised.

Forgive: Let forgiveness be a foundational piece of your love together, understanding that you are both perfectly flawed human beings who are in the process of remembering your true nature.

Dance: Yes, last but not least, dance. Literally and figuratively, dance. Approach even familiar and routine activities with each other as opportunities to dance with the divine that is alive and well within you. Even if you haven't danced in years, find out what happens when you put on some great music at home, put your arms around each other, and just see where the music takes you.

Whether you're enjoying the great heights of a new relationship or traversing the depths of a longstanding relationship, remember that the love you want is achievable. And you are worthy of this love. You were born worthy and that is an unchanging holy fact.

Like Andy, who decided early on that he wanted to have a simple love affair that lasted sixty years, you too can have a love affair that defies the odds of conventional thinking.

A Return to Innocence

True togetherness is experienced in relationship every time we reach beyond the trivial—beyond petty grievances and work-a-day distractions—and embrace the miraculous. Our relationship is instantly overflowing with blessings any time we choose to turn our eyes toward the eternal nature of our partner and ourselves. Of course, this is true in all types of relationships. Opening up to seeing the divine spirit in anyone is an acknowledgment of this brilliant truth in everyone.

Think of a particular moment when you remember noticing the divine nature of your husband, wife, partner, dear companion, or soul friend. Maybe there was nothing out of the ordinary happening; it could have been a moment at the dinner table or driving down the road together. Wherever you were and whatever you were doing, you were flooded with feelings—some of those being easy to identify, while others were achingly unnamable. And while we won't presume to know exactly what you were feeling, we will take a leap of faith to suggest that perhaps you were suddenly struck with a feeling, a sense, of *cherishing* that person—treasuring the fractal of God at your side.

This is such an exquisite feeling, isn't it? When you cherish someone, you're not only recognizing and honoring the sacredness of their being, you are *feeling* it as well. While kindness informs how you treat your beloved, cherishment is a feeling—a feeling that bypasses all the traffic of your mind, going directly from your heart to theirs. If we were allowed to slightly alter the dictionary definition of cherishment, we would want to define it as a feeling of deep valuing tinged with pure awe.

When you *feel* divine love being expressed through your partner, awe is the only thing that makes any sense.

From this field of perception, you're able to look past doubts, fears, and cynicism and remember that you're not here alone. You and your partner share a bond with the Source that brought you here—the Healer of all wounds that is bigger than the relationship itself.

The return to innocence happens every time you remember that you're standing in the garden of your life, utterly held by this invisible life force... and it is whispering to you to relax into love.

A Reflective Moment

Before you leave the meditation temple of this final chapter, take another few moments to be still and contemplate the following question:

What could you do today to acknowledge and honor the sacred in your closest relationship?

EPILOGUE
ALL AND EVERYTHING

We began our walk together, through the pages of this book, acknowledging the search for love and connection that is perhaps our deepest catalyst for growth and transformation. Each day, as we tend to our relationships—the *togetherness* we create with ourselves, our partners, children, friends, and the world we inhabit—it is love that occupies the biggest space in our hearts and minds. It is our ground, our compass, and our reason. There was once a master of language who found the perfect few words to explain why this is so.

Love is life.

All, everything that I understand,
I understand only because I love.

Everything is, everything exists, only because I love.
—LEO TOLSTOY

ACKNOWLEDGMENTS

How could we count the blessings we've received from our many friends, family members, and clients, whose personal and collective wisdom has shaped the content of this book?

Cyndi would like to especially acknowledge and thank Michael and Gabriel, her extraordinary sons, whose comprehension of love has always been more advanced than her own.

Andy would like to thank, with deep appreciation and love, Tess, his soul mate and wife for four decades. She has provided him with an exquisite model of how love is shown through her limitless devotion to Andy and their two children. Her continual support throughout this project kept his momentum going and growing.

Both Cyndi and Andy want to acknowledge three additional souls whose contribution to this book cannot even begin to be measured. First is Debra Evans, our third author, the not-so-silent voice who listened to us both and made sense of what we were saying. Debra, whose voice you actually hear in this book, is a writer and editor extraordinaire, and at this point, also a friend.

We applaud also Cyndi's manager and publishing partner, Anthony J.W. Benson, whose input, finesse, diligence and design helped create this book into one that can be loved by all those who contributed to it and to all who will read it. Then there is Will Reynolds, Deeper Well

Publishing's business partner and the owner of BRIO, whose sense of the new has led him to join hands with Cyndi and Anthony and birth a new concept into the world.

Together, all of you made this book possible, probable, and real.

ABOUT THE AUTHORS

Cyndi Dale is an internationally respected author and spiritual scholar whose books include the Gold Nautilus award-winning *The Subtle Body* and *New Chakra Healing* (reissued as *The Complete Book of Chakra Healing*, currently in its 14th printing, and *The Intuition Guidebook: How to Safely and Wisely Use Your Sixth Sense.* She is president of Life Systems Services, through which she has conducted over 35,000 client sessions and conducted trainings across Europe, Asia, and the Americas.

Cyndi has studied cross-cultural healing and energy systems and has led instructional classes in many countries, including Peru, Costa Rica, Venezuela, Japan, Belize, Mexico, Morocco, Russia and across Europe, as well as among the Lakota people and the Hawaiian kahunas. She currently lives in Minneapolis, Minnesota, with her two sons and various pets.

Andrew Wald has been a full-time psychotherapist (LCSW-C) since 1974, working with individuals, couples, families, and groups. He holds a master's in social work with a clinical specialty. Since he began his practice, Andy has logged over 50,000 therapy hours with his clients. He has received advanced certifications in Imago Relationship Therapy, Gestalt Therapy, and Neuro-Linguistic Programming.

His wife of 39 years and their two children live in Chevy Chase, Maryland.

Debra Evans is a freelance writer, editor, and writing coach who has worked with renowned authors and teachers, including Debbie Ford, Nicole Daedone, and Barnet Bain. As former National Director of Conference Programming for Whole Life Expos, Debra has worked with *New York Times* best-selling authors, including Wayne Dyer, Deepak Chopra, and Marianne Williamson.

Debra lives in the San Francisco Bay area where she relishes foggy summer days and a close community of friends who share her passion of transformation.

Another Must-Have Book by Cyndi Dale

The Intuition Guidebook provides help for those who feel they are "too sensitive," hearing things no one else hears, seeing things that aren't there, having dreams that come true—in other words, psychic. Dale leads readers through the gifts involved with being psychically sensitive, where each of these gifts comes from, and how to control them. Highlights are exercises to find psychic sensitivities, establishing guardians and focus upon protecting oneself and transitioning from sensitivity to psychic intuitive.

The Intuition Guidebook: *How to Safely and Wisely Use Your Sixth Sense*
ISBN: 978-0-9826687-9-5
U.S. $16.95 / Deeper Well Publishing & BRIO Press

Also by Cyndi Dale

Books

The Intuition Guidebook: How to Safely and Wisely Use Your Sixth Sense
(Deeper Well Publishing, 2011)

Kundalini: Divine Energy, Divine Life
(Llewellyn Worldwide, 2011)

The Everyday Clairvoyant
(Llewellyn Worldwide, 2010)

The Complete Book of Chakra Healing
(Llewellyn Worldwide, 2009; formerly *New Chakra Healing*)

The Subtle Body: An Encyclopedia of Your Energetic Anatomy
(Sounds True, 2009)

Illuminating the Afterlife
(Sounds True, 2008)

Attracting Your Perfect Body Through the Chakras
(Crossing Press, 2006)

Advanced Chakra Healing: Heart Disease; The Four Pathways Approach
(Crossing Press, 2006)

Advanced Chakra Healing: Energy Mapping on the Four Pathways
(Crossing Press, 2005)

Advanced Chakra Healing: Cancer; The Four Pathways Approach
(Crossing Press, 2005)

Attracting Prosperity Through the Chakras
(Crossing Press, 2004)

E-books (available at www.cyndidale.com)
The Energy of You: Your Chakras

DVDs and CDs
*Energetic Boundaries: How to Stay Protected and
Connected in Work, Love, and Life* (Sounds True, 2011)
Energy Clearing (Sounds True, 2009)
Healing Across Space & Time (Sounds True, 2009)
Advanced Chakra Wisdom (Sounds True, 2008)
Illuminating the Afterlife (Sounds True, 2008)
The Songbird Series (Essential Energy, 2008)